C L R JAMES

C L R James

Cricket's Philosopher King

Dave Renton

HAUS BOOKS
London

Copyright © 2007 Dave Renton

First published in Great Britain in 2007 by Haus Publishing,
26 Cadogan Court, Draycott Avenue, London SW3 3BX
www.hauspublishing.co.uk

The moral rights of the author have been asserted

A CIP catalogue record for this book is available from the British Library

ISBN 978-1-905791-01-9

Typeset in Garamond by MacGuru Ltd
info@macguru.org.uk

Printed and bound by Graphicom in Vicenza, Italy
Jacket illustration: Getty Images

Contents

Introduction

(Previous page) England vs the West Indies at the Oval, 24 August 1963. England skipper Ted Dexter is caught out in England's second innings in the fifth and final Test.

For more than 40 years, and certainly since the appearance of his great book, *Beyond a Boundary*, C L R James has been known as the cricketing Marxist.[1] The term is too narrow to grasp James' genius, but it does some justice to the paradoxical character of his life. For when we think of cricket, we conceive of the game of Empire: the sport that today joins England and her former colonies, Australia, Bangladesh, India, New Zealand, Pakistan, South Africa, Sri Lanka and the West Indies.* With its special language and arcane laws, cricket appears to be the product of some antique past. Ask the average person to position cricket on a political scale, from left to right, and most would place it unthinkingly to the right of centre. If the persistence of cricket in a world of string theory and superconductors is the sign of some anachronism, then how strange to find a cricketing Marxist, the champion of protest, caught slumbering on a deckchair at Lord's.

A moment's thought shows that the supposed paradox is no such thing. Cricket may have been pastoral in societies where the great majority of people lived on the land, but today its centres are all in the cities. As a spectacle, in the make-up of its audience and in the experiences outside the game of those who have played it, cricket in England in 1800 was in all important respects different from cricket in the Caribbean in 1900 or in Australia in 1950 or in South Africa today. Real historical imagination is required to recall, for example, that as recently as the 1920s and 1930s, English cricketers were divided into two camps: amateurs and professionals. Amateurs entered grounds through separate changing rooms. Almost all county captains were amateur. In the 1920s most professionals seemed to accept the system. The England batsman Jack Hobbs always deferred to amateur captains and described any criticism of them as 'bolshieness'. Inwardly, however, all professionals could see the moments at which the behaviour of certain amateurs shaded into hucksterism (how else were any financially insecure children of the middle classes supposed

---

* The Interim Committee of Zimbabwe Cricket withdrew from Test cricket in January 2006.

to keep going, except by keeping a close eye on the family business?): as when Percy Fender, for example, used his status as captain of Surrey to promote his wine-dealing firm. Anyone could follow a good captain, but one without talent, or one leading to some sporting catastrophe? In such conditions, and under the pressure of a decade of slump and dictatorship, we should not be surprised by the capacity of cricket (as during the 1932 Bodyline crisis) to show the character of war.

Give the game a global reach, or the beginnings of it, and everything we take for granted is susceptible to change: from the width and composition of the strip on which the players compete, to the size of the ground or of the competing teams, the duration of an over, the choice of materials to make a bat or a ball. Just in our own time, we can see that cricket played with tennis balls on the streets of Bradford is not the same game as Tests played over five days at Lord's. In 1993, Sri Navas Rana dominated Nepal's premier one-day competition, the Rameshwore Memorial trophy. Eight thousand people watched the series final. As man of the tournament Rana was awarded ... a colour television set. In 1996, India's Sachin Tendulkar signed a sponsorship deal worth more than a million pounds a year. You could fly from Tendulkar's Bombay to Rana's Kathmandu in less than five hours, but in cricketing terms, they were the whole world apart. To paraphrase Marx: people play cricket not in circumstances of their own choosing, but in conditions encountered, given and transmitted from the past. Made and remade by its players and spectators, cricket belongs to all: to the future and to the past, to the left just as well as to the right.

As for Marxism, here too we must scrape through a muck of encrusted cliché. In the 1930s, the Scott Tissue Towel Company of Philadelphia advertised its washroom products to the good employers of North America through a poster with the heading, 'Is Your Washroom Breeding Bolsheviks?' Purchase better-quality toilet paper, it was suggested, and even the most aggressive Marxist would be satisfied. The poster showed a typical radical: moustachioed, ugly and grimacing: at odds with himself, his boss and with life. Against this visual image of permanent choler, this book set the life of C L R James, described in the following terms by his publisher Frederick Warburg: 'Immensely amiable, he loved the flesh-pots of capitalism, fine cooking, fine clothes, fine furniture and beautiful women, without a trace of the guilty remorse to be expected from a seasoned warrior of the class war.'[2] James was in fact a radical where radicalism was needed, and at other times content; a patient, humorous and cultured man.

More than this, C L R James was one of the most original thinkers of the 20th century, equally at home in writing about art, history, literature, politics, philosophy or (yes) sport. Among those who write broadly, some find themselves conquered by the brilliance of their subject. With each book they begin, you feel that they start anew. Not so with James; his personality was constant, his sensibility unique. Among his most ardent followers, James was described in his own lifetime as the black Plato, the black Hegel. Edward Said dubbed him 'the father of modern Caribbean writing'.[3]

Of all of James' interests, however, it is cricket that catches the imagination and stands at the centre of this book. For if James' life has a mystery, so too does the sport to which he was attached. While cricket today is a game of the cities, its past was indeed rural. To use the Jamesian metaphor, its origins were at first bounded, before they could be escaped. Two hundred and thirty years ago, competitive cricket was dominated not by a city or a county, but by a single village in sleepy Hampshire: Hambledon, who in 1777 took on All England, beating that national team by an innings and 168 runs. The Marylebone Cricket Club (MCC) was formed ten years later.[4] One hundred years later, cricket in England was shaped above all by the personality of W G Grace, a figure to whom James, as cricket's great historian, was attracted. Grace's led his team, the Gentlemen, brutally against the Professionals. He was also the epitome of the paid amateur, demanding twice in expenses what his professional rivals were allowed in fees. Against the narrowness of its early history, what is it about cricket that has enabled it to play such a wide role: finding followers from Iceland to the South Pole, appealing to ANC cadres in the prisons of apartheid, just as much as to their jailors, chafing for their part at what they judged the iniquity of the sporting boycott? James reflected on this question more deeply than anyone. On his death, *Wisden* (usually and lazily termed cricket's bible: more accurately it is the game's *hadith*: its tradition) described *Beyond a Boundary* as 'the greatest book on the game yet written'.[5] True, but why? One answer is that James was a profoundly autobiographical writer. All historians are, but James exceptionally so. It helped that his biography was more interesting than most. In the range of places he had lived and the things he had believed and done, James had enjoyed such a wide set of experiences that he could see cricket from both outside and in. He had a privileged access to the game.

One hope of this book is to persuade Marxists of the joys of cricket, and followers of cricket of the calibre of James and of James' Marxism. It is a disturbing lapse in radical theory that there are not more writers setting out urgently to explain the triumph of Brian Lara's 375 or the bathos of his 400, the success of Flintoff and Pietersen's charge against Lee and Kasprowicz at Edgbaston in 2005, the contrast between the weight of India within the sport's upper echelons and the underperformance (until recently) of the national Test side. A modest example illustrates the general point: at the end of the second Ashes Test in December 2006, with his team set for a series victory, Australian batsman Damien Martyn suddenly and at some financial cost to himself retired both from Test cricket and from all levels of the game. Would it not have been easier to keep his place? Even if he had played badly, would he not have shared in the collective glory of success? Thinking in the aftermath of the player's decision, we can speculate as to flaws in his temperament, of weaknesses that perhaps he already realised, but which were only now in the last moments of his career becoming obvious to wider numbers of people. We can think also of age, and the effect it eventually has on all physical prowess. James, you can be sure, would have found in this moment a lesson of general applicability. Part of the pleasure of all sport, he would say, comes from the sensation it imparts in the watcher of inevitability. The winners win, always, that is what they do. For those backing the losing side, this necessity shapes the routine grind of spectating. Cricket, with its five-day tests and five-Test series, gives plenty of chances for superiority to show. But some times the inevitable is cheated. Teams or players improve. The weather plays its part. Shocks can occur on the pitch or off, and yes, Martyn's resignation was a surprise.

If Marxists are unwilling to think the language of sport, of cricket, and of football too, and of all the other games in which millions spend their leisure, then for whom do we have any right to speak? And conversely: cricket's supporters too deserve a literature that treats them as adults, which integrates their own complex views of nationality, culture, society, art and history, and connects them all to the game that they love. In James' hands, Marxism was uniquely well-placed to join up the dots. To make those who followed cricket Marxists, to teach Marxists to love cricket: that was a part of his life's work.

As a schoolboy, the young James claimed to have found in the game a code of ethics to guide his later life. He loved cricket as he idealised the society that had given birth to the sport. But cricket was the affair of his youth and political change the passion of his adult years. Born in 1901 a subject of the British Queen, reaching maturity in the 1920s at a time when Britain was in decline, James' identification with the values of the game led him to challenge the world both in rejection of the empire's continuing strength, including chiefly its support of race and class privilege, and for its weakness, taking in its failure to hold firm in the face of its great power rivals. Britain lacked both generosity and firmness. It could not play the game even by its own rules. Having judged the empire corrupt and having insisted on the absolute right of his fellow Trinidadians to rule themselves, James did not stop there. He continued by offering his support to every nationality desiring independence, to black against white, to the poor against the rich, and to the oppressed everywhere. Such was the cricketing Marxist. It is hard not to wonder what his Oxford-educated teachers would have made of their once meek pupil.

1

The Making of a Writer

(Previous page) W G Grace (1848–1915). James dedicated his book *Beyond a Boundary* to Grace, Learie Constantine and Frank Worrell.

Cyril Lionel Robert James was born in Trinidad on 4 January 1901 and grew up in a town called Tunapuna. Later in life, James reflected on his youth. His brother Eric had been 'feckless', his aunts Florence and Lottie 'stern and puritanical'. James' mother Ida Elizabeth 'Bessie' Rudder was 'a very tall woman, my colour, with a superb carriage and so handsome that everybody always asked who she was'.[6] Above all else, 'she was a reader. She read everything that came her way. I can see her now, sitting very straight with the book held high, her pince-nez on her Caucasian nose, reading till long after midnight. If I got up there she was, reading, the book still held high. As she read and put it down I picked it up.' James' father, Robert James, was a teacher. An accomplished cricketer, he had also taught himself music and shorthand.[7] On the occasion of James' fourth birthday, his father gave him a bat and ball, 'and never afterwards was I without them both for long'. As soon as his brother Eric could walk, James would attempt to involve him in games of garden cricket. Eric for his part only liked batting: as soon as he was out he would throw the bat to the ground and refuse to play any further. 'He cheated naturally and I was naturally honest.'[8] James looked to the older generation. His father Robert had played for Tunapuna, where he acquired a reputation for hitting sixes over extra cover, no easy stroke. But his interest in the sport waned, following the arrival of a wife and then children. Robert had taken himself from humble origins, the son of a pan-boiler on a sugar estate. Bessie's father Josh Rudder had been the first black driver on the Trinidad Railway. Three of James' grandparents had come as migrants to Trinidad from Barbados. 'Nobody in the Caribbean,' James would write, 'is native to the environment.'[9] Robert and Jessie met in church and married there. As well as Cyril and Eric, they had a daughter, Olive.

The young James' earliest years were spent in the rural south of Trinidad with his father. On completing their training, teachers were required to work in village schools before they could transfer to the towns. For nearly a decade, James' family divided their time between Tunapuna and North Trace, where Robert taught. The population of North Trace comprised cane cutters brought first from India to Trinidad as indentured labourers. The town contained a mosque, a temple and a church. The school year lasted just six months, so as not to interfere with the sugar-cutting season. Classes in the school held up to a hundred at a time, and much of the teaching was by rote. The school building was cramped, and the family home was hardly more spacious. James later recalled that the house had contained just two rooms, measuring in total 12 feet by 18 feet. There were holes in the floor and even in the thatched roof.[10]

As well as the home in North Trace, the family also kept a grander house in Tunapuna, then a small town of around 3,000 people, situated eight miles outside Port of Spain. James would live there for six months of the year, with his grandmother and his aunts. One effect of his frequent migrations between town and countryside was to break down James' sense of belonging. From a sense that no setting was fixed, James also learned to dream, to imagine other places and times.

The young James developed his imagination in part by watching sport. One early memory was of a horse race. Years later, he could recall the details of the landscape, the character of the competitors, the shifting emotions of the crowd as an older horse emerged from the pack to snatch victory right at the last.[11]

The family home overlooked the grounds of Tunapuna Cricket Club. In his memoir, *Beyond a Boundary,* James would later recall the proximity of the two. 'An umpire could have stood at the bedroom window.' One day, James watched the club's star batsman Arthur Jones. 'Nearly every over he was getting up on his toes and cutting away.' But the wicket was wet and the ball would not run to the boundary. Sensing Jones' frustration, the fielding team began to bowl short. Down came a bouncer, and Jones lashed hard. 'There was the usual shout,' James recalled, 'a sudden silence and another shout, not so loud this time. Then from my window I saw Jones walking out and people began to walk away. He had been caught by point standing with his back to the barbed wire.' James found the confusion and subsequent despair of the moment overpowering: 'I could not see it from my window and I asked and asked until I was told what had happened. I knew that something out of the ordinary had happened to us who were watching. We had been lifted to the heights and cast down into the depths in much less than a fraction of a second. Countless as are the times that this experience has been repeated, most often in the company of tens of thousands of people, I have never lost the zest of wondering at it and pondering over it.'[12]

Many years later, the novelist V S Naipaul* observed that cricket achieved its sovereignty in the West Indies because it represented style, grace and other elements of culture in a society that had little else of its kind. Reading his then friend's words, James seized on them, and wrote back regretting that he had never said the same.[13] But we should not endorse Naipaul's judgment too quickly. It contains hints of the younger author's patrician disdain. James' attitude towards popular culture was more sympathetic. In the Trinidad of James' youth, other openings could also be found, beyond cricket. 'I was fascinated by the calypso singers and the sometimes ribald ditties they sang in their tents during carnival time. But, like many of the black middle class, to my mother a calypso was a matter for ne'er-do-wells and at best the common people. I was made to understand that the road to the calypso tent was the road to hell, and there were always plenty of examples of hell's inhabitants to whom she could point.'[14]

After cricket, James' other joy was literature. From his mother, James learned to read widely. From his father, James did not yet acquire self-discipline but a consciousness of its need. 'I learnt discrimination from my father. He was no reader, except for books connected with his teaching, but as a man of some education he knew who, if not what, the classics

---

* Vidiadhar Surajprasad Naipaul (1932–) was born in Trinidad, the son of the author Seepersad Naipaul, and the descendant of Indian indentured labourers. He arrived in England in the 1950s where he was for a time a friend and admirer of James. His novels include *The Mystic Masseur* (1957), *A House for Mr Biswas* (1961), *Mr Stone and the Knights Companion* (1963), *A Flag on the Island* (1967), *In a Free State* (1971), *Guerrillas* (1975), and *A Bend in the River* (1979). In 2001, he was awarded the Nobel Prize for Literature.

were.'[15] Under his parents' dual influence, the youthful scholar was encouraged to read Aeschylus, Balzac, the Brontë sisters, Dickens, Dostoyevsky, Hawthorne, Kipling, Scott, Thackeray and Tolstoy. 'Thackeray, not Marx,' James would insist, 'bears the heaviest responsibility for me.'[16] It was Thackeray's emphasis on English stiff upper lips and moral self-reliance that appealed.

'I was a bright boy. A very bright boy,' James would later write.[17] His reading was chosen by his parents to inspire in him a love of British culture, a belief in the civilising mission of the mother country. James' mother Bessie kept an illustrated edition of the complete works of Shakespeare. 'Now I could not read a play of Shakespeare but I remember perfectly looking up the Act and Scenes stated at the foot of the illustration and reading that particular scene. I am quite sure that before I was seven I had read all those scenes. I read neither before or after, but if the picture told me Act 3, Scene 4, I would look it up and fortified myself with the picture.' Not all James' reading was highbrow. He also read *The Review of Reviews*, *Comic Cuts* and *Strand Magazine*.[18]

James was struck by the contrast between his own quiet life in Trinidad and the conflicts he found in literature. Yet Trinidad may not have been quite as tranquil as it seemed. The island was a possession of the British Empire. The abolition of slavery had happened in living memory. James himself was the great-grandson of slaves.[19] The society was still marked by open racism. One instance of the collective stupidity meant something to James, then and later. The island's best cricketers were black, and yet the West Indies' captain was always white. As it was in sport, so it was in every other aspect of life: positions were fixed. Even a middle-class family such as James' could aspire to security only through exceptional hard work, in each successive generation. Yet ruled by Britain, the subjects of the colony could hardly have been unaware of movements elsewhere for independence. A Trinidadian, Henry Sylvester Williams, founded the first Pan African Congress in London in 1900. The British were soon caught up in their long war in South Africa. Another European power, Russia, suffered an embarrassing military defeat at the hands of Japan in 1904–5, when James was aged just three and four.

A definite hierarchy shaped life on the island. In another tale from *Beyond a Boundary*, James described his grandmother's and his aunt's contempt for their neighbours, the Bondmans. They considered the two Bondman children Matthew and Marie shameless, sexual beasts. Matthew was a young adult when James first met him, 'medium height and size, and an awful character. He was generally dirty. He would not work. His eyes were fierce, his language was violent and his voice was loud. His lips curled back naturally and he intensified it by an almost permanent snarl'. Bondman was the personification of the fears of the middle class, that without reading and cleanliness, they too would be sucked back down into the world of the urban poor. For James, the story was rather more complex. 'Matthew, so crude and vulgar in every aspect of his life, with a bat in his hand was all grace and style. When he practised on an afternoon with the local club people stayed to watch and walked away when he was finished.'[20]

In 1910, James was entered for a scholarship to the celebrated Queen's Royal College. Competing against other students, 'fighting cocks' most of them two years his senior, and who entered the hall beside their willing parents, James came first. It was a great prize. Only four scholarships were on offer each year. Founded in 1870, the school had been established for the children of British settlers. It was now opening up to local children, the sons of independent planters and of some teachers. The main building, known as the Main Block, was one of the celebrated sights of Trinidad. Designed in the German Renaissance style, it featured royal palms, a tall, lighted tower and a chiming clock. Entering the school for the first time must have given James an extraordinary thrill. He was to remain at Queen's for the next eight years. It was then that Trinidad seemed quiet to him and the world outside most exciting.

James' teens were the years of the 1914–18 war, a conflict to which the colonies were expected to contribute, a West Indies Battalion fighting for the British in France.[21] The war culminated in the defeat of Germany, in the formation of the League of Nations, in American President Woodrow Wilson's promises of self-government to the small nations, and in the Russian Revolution. One Tunapuna friend was Malcolm Nurse, who later went by the name of George Padmore.* Nurse was born the year after James, and was like him the son of a teacher. His father, James Alfonso Nurse, was one of the best-read men that the young James met. He even wrote letters on scientific matters for the local press. When his correspondence was discovered, however, his employers judged that Nurse had ambitions above his station. He was compelled to resign, adopting Islam in protest against his treatment and becoming the first black Muslim on the island. Malcolm and the young James used to bathe together in summer in the river Arima.

Queen's was modelled on an English private education. The nine teachers were all graduates of public schools and Oxford or Cambridge. The curriculum included Latin, Greek, French, Mathematics, English grammar and history. The authorities taught James to think that a good man was disciplined, consistent and subject to the same rules that he asked others to observe. These rules were not taught abstractly but through sport.

James, in turn, was fascinated by cricket, 'I analysed strokes, I studied types, I read its history, its beginnings, how and when it changed from period to period, I read about it in Australia and in South Africa. I read

---

* Born Malcolm Nurse, George Padmore (1902–59) left Trinidad for America, studying at New York University and Harvard Law School. He joined the Communist Party and took Padmore as his party name. He was invited to Russia, where he was appointed Secretary of the International Trade Union Committee of Negro Workers, with responsibility for encouraging independence movements in Third World. But the leaders of the Soviet Union began to argue for alliances with Britain and France, causing them to retreat on their previous support for the subjects of empire. Padmore resigned his positions and moved to London, where he met up again with James and worked with him in establishing an International African Services Bureau, a meeting-place for the future leaders of the independent African states.

and compared statistics, I made clippings, I talked to all cricketers, particularly the inter-colonial cricketers and those who had gone abroad. I
compared what they told me with what I read in old copies of *Wisden*.
I looked up the play of the men who had done well or badly against
the West Indies. I read and appreciated the phraseology of the laws.'[22]
Through literature, James learned more of the sport's history. In *The
Pickwick Papers*, he discovered, 'Dickens refers easily to a cricket match
played in the West Indies by two British officers. Trinidad became British
only in 1797, yet in 1842, not ten years after the abolition of slavery,
there was a well established Trinidad Cricket Club. By 1891, there was
an intercolonial tournament between Barbados, Jamaica and what has
now become British Guiana. In 1894–5 the first English team visited
the West Indies.'[23]

One of the idiosyncrasies of the British public school system is the
very heavy emphasis that it places on two opposite conditions: first,
on spending years as a junior, in which the sole demand is of subaltern
loyalty, and then on a brief period of seniority, in which the older boys
are expected to lead the young. Both emphases are deliberate: as a junior,
you are expected to endure a range of leadership styles, several of them
unpleasant. Unless you have suffered many years of arbitrary, personal
domination, it is suggested, you cannot know how to lead later in a
fashion that is more generous.

As a result of winning the scholarship a year early, James was young
when he started at Queen's. He spent eight years at the grammar school:
one more than each of his contemporaries. For years, he was one of the
most junior boys, trained to look upwards and admire. Then suddenly
James was a senior boy. It was his turn to lead. In his own account of the
period, James refers obliquely to one or perhaps two roles of authority
that he held in various school cricket teams. 'I never gave to a friend a vote
or a place, which by any stretch of imagination could be seen as belonging to an enemy or to a stranger.'[24] To speak of having a vote is to suggest
that senior boys held some collegial power over selection. To speak of
giving a place is to suggest that James was at one point a team captain. If

so, then his task would have been to choose the other players for his team, to inspire them, to lead them on and off the pitch. We can understand then the emphasis he put on studying the history of the game: because he *taught* it to others. He internalised the school's moral code.

Cricket took up a great deal of the school day: what were the pupils supposed to learn from it? In the Queen's system, cricket played a dual role. The laws of cricket were fixed. The umpires (chosen from the teaching staff) guarded order. Their decisions were final. Yet if cricket served to uphold hierarchy, it could do so only by concealing its own strangeness. Cricket has been treated often as a metaphor for life. If so, then 'life' is a curious thing. Followers of other sports such as football may assume that cricket inhabits a rational, ordered world, like their own. It does not. A football pitch must be of limited specification, the goal of a certain size. The game lasts for 90 minutes and then, barring exceptions, it ends. Not so with cricket. A match of Test cricket as often lasts for three or four days as for five (its maximum duration). Let the opening side bat disastrously, and a one-innings school game scheduled for several hours might be over before lunch. Cricket is amongst other things a permanent competition between the batsman (whoever happens to be batting just at the time) and the bowler (again, irrespective of who has the ball). Make the pitch flat and even, and batsmen on both teams will prosper. Prepare an uneven surface, or play on a grey overcast day, and the ball will jag about, bowlers will succeed. Not in football, nor in rugby, nor in hockey, nor in baseball, nor in any of the other team sports does so much turn on the pitch, nor on that day's climate.

Characterised by both order and disorder, cricket can at times be a meritocratic sport. In any team, the average scores of a batsman or the total wickets taken by a bowler can be counted. The skilled and the diligent prove themselves. Favourites may be chosen, but will not prosper. Nepotism is 'just not cricket'.[25] There can be no more a hereditary batsman or bowler than there can be a hereditary poet.

Cricket tends to reinforce a social system most clearly in one of two situations: first, in a society of fixed order, where the prosperous are guaranteed a condition of luxury, so that they are indeed fitter, happier and better rested than any rivals. In such conditions, a sporting hierarchy will indeed confirm the order of life. Secondly, cricket and society can reinforce one another in a world of freedom where talent and industry are given free hand to try whatever they liked. Here, too, the cricketing hierarchy, or, more accurately, its absence, will mirror the freedom of the world outside.

We should therefore read James' frequent declarations of love for the game as more complex than they first appear. The cricket he learned at school, James later insisted, was the medium of his entire philosophy. Under its influence, he absorbed a moral code, one that he long retained, 'I never cheated, I never appealed for a decision unless I thought the batsman was out, I never argued with the umpire, I never jeered at a defeated opponent … If I caught myself complaining or making excuses I pulled up. If afterwards I remembered doing it I took an inward decision to try not to do it again. From the eight years of school life this code became the moral framework of my existence. It has never left me.'[26] Nothing in James' account implies undue deference to authority. It speaks rather of a contract between player and opponent, or between both and the game.

While cricket rose in his affection, James tired of books. 'I paid no attention to the curriculum.' His rebellion, if we can call it that, was the protest of an intelligent person with no challenge in the classroom. It is revealing that of all the various teachers of his youth, James recalled few with any vividness, except one, the principal of the college, a Mr Burslem. 'No more devoted, conscientious and self-sacrificing official ever worked in the colonies … he would write mitigating words in my report, call me to do some personal task for him (a way of showing favour) and in the course of it try to show me the error of my ways. He did it constantly with me and other waywards. He was a man with a belief in the rod, which he combined with a choleric and autocratic disposition. But he was loved by generations of boys and held in respectful admiration through the colony.'[27]

Following his previous success in the scholarship exam, James might have been expected to graduate from his first award to a second bursary. There were three island scholarships worth £600 each, which enabled the brightest pupils to study law or medicine abroad, typically at Oxford or Cambridge, and return to the island with a profession, made for life. Yet James neglected his studies. 'My distracted father lectured me, punished me, flogged me. I would make good resolutions, do well for one term and fall from grace again.'[28]

The headmaster Mr Burslem reported James to the school governors as a failing student and threatened to withdraw his bursary. A family conference was convened. James was instructed to catch the first train home at the end of his lessons and play no more cricket. We can imagine a shocked gathering of James' extended family. His father was a teacher. His godparents were teachers. Most of his parents' friends were teachers. If James' scholarship were to be removed, his failure would be reported in the local press. His idleness threatened to undermine several years of collective effort towards a social peak. Yet even now there could be no meeting of minds between the older generation and the younger. It was cricket that James loved. Faced with strict instructions from his family, James held to his higher calling, and continued to play the game. It does not seem to have occurred to the young James that dishonesty of this sort was barely compatible with the moral code of cricket that he claimed to espouse. 'I forged letters, I borrowed flannels, I borrowed money to pay my fare, I borrowed bicycles to ride to the matches and borrowed money to repay them. I was finally entangled in such a web of lies, forged letters, borrowed clothes and borrowed money that it was no wonder that my family looked on me as a sort of trial from heaven.' James' father beat him repeatedly; and into his thirties, James would dream a continuing nightmare, in which he returned home a failure to await his father's wrath.[29]

James was conscious of his own intelligence and capacity for reading. He simply lacked the means to apply these skills in class, in a way that made him feel alive. Robert James finally conceded, and agreed to let his son concentrate on the game. James never did win the scholarship to Oxford, but left Queen's in 1918.

In the subsequent years, James was employed as a teacher, first oddly enough at Queen's Royal College. How was he, of all possible teachers, supposed to develop habits of industry in his pupils? It was James the team player, the school presumably chose to employ, not James the former dilatory student. One of his pupils at Queen's in the 1920s was Eric Williams,* later the first Prime Minister of the independent Trinidad and Tobago. James taught next at the Government Training College. Photographs from the late 1920s show him to have been a smartly-dressed young man in a light suit and spotted tie. His posture is erect and his hair cropped. His face and body are recognisable as those of the later author.[30] Yet the personality he would adopt still remained to be formed.

James played cricket through his teens. His performances are recorded into the early 1930s.' 'By the time I left school at the age of eighteen I was a good defensive bat and could have held my own in any English public-school side. I could bowl fast medium with a high action, swing the ball late from leg and break it with shoulder-and-finger action from the off. I was looked upon as one of the coming players on the island ... I have at various times dismissed for small scores St Hill, Small, Constantine, Wiles and other Test players and in my best days would have opened the bowling cheerfully against any batsman I have seen.'[31] Through the 1920s, James played regularly and at a high level. He performed first for

---

* Eric Williams (1911–81) was a historian and later a career politician. Born the son of a civil servant, Williams was educated at Queen's Royal College and there won an island scholarship, allowing him to attend Oxford University where he received his doctorate in 1938. Williams then taught at Howard University, returning to Trinidad to serve on an Anglo-American Caribbean Commission. Breaking with the Commission, he became a leading public spokesman of Caribbean independence. He was later the first Prime Minister of Trinidad and Tobago, remaining in that position from 1956 until his death. Williams invited James to Trinidad to work for his movement. His and James' short-lived alliance in Trinidad is discussed below.

Old Collegians, averaging more than 70 with the bat in a side that won the island's second-division championship. It became evident that James should progress, and in particular that he should choose one of the first-division teams. The decision was protracted and James would treat it afterwards to careful scrutiny.*

Four sides were closed to James, Queen's Park Club was the preserve of wealthy whites; Shamrock was Catholic and again predominantly white; Constabulary was as the name suggests a police club; while Stingo was the club of the talented, black poor. There were two remaining clubs open to him. Maple was normally the team of the Asian middle class. A doctor with dark skin would normally find the side closed to him, but a lighter-skinned department-store clerk might have been able to join. Shannon played a similar role for the black lower middle class.

James turned to a friend of his father's for advice, and was told: 'Many of the Maple boys are your friends and mine. These are the people you are going to meet in life. Join them; it will be better in the end.' So while James might have been expected to choose Shannon, he sided instead with Maple. The choice might be put down to residual family loyalty, or even to ambition on James' part, for what better sign could there be of social mobility, on this colour-divided island, than to social-ise with those of a lighter skin? 'Faced with the fundamental divisions

---

* 'Between 1900 and 1939 the development of West Indian society improved the status and conditions of the coloured middle classes with effective results in the organisation of cricket as a national expression ... Clubs played every Sunday in club competitions and not infrequently a white member of the Legislative Council or President of the Chamber of Commerce would be playing amicably for his club against another most of whose members were black porters, messengers or other members of the lowest social classes. In addition to clubs exclusively white, with perhaps a few coloured men of wealth or distinction, the brown-skinned middle class also formed their own clubs. So did the black-skinned middle class. In time the black plebeians also formed their own. These divisions, not always in every island ironclad, were not only understood but accepted by players and populations alike.' C L R James, 'Cricket in West Indian Culture', *New Society* (6 June 1963).

in the island,' James later accepted, he sided not with the left but with 'the right'.[32] In pure cricketing terms, this decision turned out to be a bad mistake. Maple lost to Shannon nine times in the next ten years. Shannon acquired a number of players who would become Test cricketers. James was separated from a rising generation, including above all his future friend Learie Constantine.* For a decade, James was a successful club cricketer. He was not picked, however, for any higher level. Thus cricket became for him a part-time pursuit. James failed to reach the top of the sporting ladder, falling short by several rungs.

James now saw the need to develop a second vocation. To his friends, he now insisted that his name would be made as a writer. James attended plays and concerts, and as early as 1919 he took part in a literary circle, the Maverick Club.

James' first published works were short stories. One, 'La Divina Pastora', appeared in 1927, and was published in the British *Saturday Review*. The story tells of Anita Perez, a young woman on a cocoa plantation who is desperate to secure the affections of her lover, Sebastian Montagnio. She offers to an image of the Madonna her golden chain, her only valuable possession. The lover becomes anxious at her departure from the previous, relaxed conventions of their courtship. At the end of

---

* Learie Nicholas Constantine (1901–71) was the son of Lebrun Constantine, a cricketer who had also represented the West Indies. An opening bowler and a middle-order batsman, Learie Constantine made his name first with the Caribbean side that toured England in 1928, and then as a professional for Nelson in the Lancashire League. Constantine's proudest moment came at Georgetown, in 1930, when West Indies beat England for the first time. He was not the only member of the team to excel, George Headley made a major batting contribution; but it was Constantine who twice broke the English batting with figures of four for 35 and five for 87. These figures were not approached by any other bowler in the game. He was a *Wisden* Cricketer of the Year in 1940. After retiring from cricket, he became a commentator for the BBC. He studied law and was called to the bar in 1954. Later he returned to Trinidad, serving in Eric Williams' government. After independence, he was his country's first High Commissioner in London. He later died in England.

the story, the chain is returned miraculously to her dresser. This story shows a deep willingness to grasp the narrow existence into which many women of the author's generation were trapped. As James writes of his protagonist: 'She lived one earthly aim. She considered it her duty and her business to be married as quickly as possible, first because in that retired spot it marked the sweet perfection of a woman's existence, and secondly, because feminine youth and beauty, if they exist, fade early on in the hard work on the cocoa plantation ... She had no thought of women's rights nor any Ibsenic theories of morality.'[33]

A second story, 'Turner's Prosperity', concerns a young, indebted clerk, while James' third published piece, 'Triumph', describes love in the barrack-yards of Trinidad. 'In the corner of one yard,' James wrote, 'is the hopelessly inadequate water-closet, unmistakable to the nose if not the eye; sometimes there is a structure with the title of bathroom, a courtesy title, for he or she who would wash in it with decent privacy must cover the person as if bathing on the banks of the Thames; the kitchen happily presents no difficulty; never is there one and each barrack-yarder cooks before her door. In the centre there is a pile of stones.'[34] The latter two stories appeared in *Trinidad*, a magazine published by James with his friend Alfred Mendes in Christmas 1929. After two issues, *Trinidad* merged into another magazine *The Beacon*, edited by another friend, Albert Gomes, from 1931. In May 1931, *The Beacon* published a short fictional piece by James called simply, 'Revolution'. A conversation with an imaginary exiled Venezuelan revolutionary, the story recounts an uprising of the people defeated by the cowardice of its leaders.[35]

Even while James had relinquished his original plan to play cricket professionally, he was continuing to collect scraps of sporting folklore to generate notes on games, compiling the details that would inform his later journalism. He followed the results of the touring overseas sides. Until 1928, London judged the West Indies teams to be unworthy of international or Test status. London itself was still ostensibly the realm of gentlemen amateurs. Touring sides were sent not as England elevens but in the name of the Marylebone Cricket Club, whose headquarters were at Lord's. When an MCC team visited the West Indies in 1930, James would write later, 'West Indies had perked up enough to win the series. Roach had fulfilled all its early promise and George Hedley of Jamaica took the field. Only twenty years of age, he made a century three times and practically won the Test at Georgetown against time on a wearing wicket.' Success in 1930 seemed to prove that the Caribbean side had stepped up in quality but the next away tour, of Australia, gave less ground for hope. 'Woodfall's team was too much for them. The side never caught itself until the last State match against New South Wales. The tour was saved from inconsequence by the full blossoming of Headley, who was hailed by the best judges in critical Australia as a batsman *sans peur et sans reproche*.'[36]

In 1927, James married Juanita Samuel Young. According to James' second wife, 'Juanita was of Spanish and Chinese descent; from Venezuela ... Theirs was a traditional West Indian marriage. She was to keep the house in order, cook, and be his bedmate when he desired ... He described his relationship with Juanita as "pleasant". She, on the other hand, told [James] that the only time he paid her any attention was when he was on top of her. On weekends he would gather up the gramophone, records and book and they would take themselves to Tunapuna to stay with his mother and father. Juanita became pregnant, but nearing term the baby died as a result of the umbilical cord twisted around its neck. [James] did not seem particularly saddened, only describing their infant as a fine looking baby boy.'[37] James' seeming lack of grief may have meant only that he lacked the capacity to express sadness. There would be other, later silences.

The novelist George Lamming describes James' origins as follows, 'a peasant by recent origin, a colonial by education, [he was] a Victorian with the rebel seed'.[38] The word 'seed' is well chosen: it suggests blossoming in stages. We should not exaggerate the speed of James' conversion to rebellion. By the late 1920s, he was a prominent member of Trinidad's bohemian set. Even now, however, his horizons were still limited. His ambition was to make his name on the cricket fields of Trinidad and in its public libraries. Thus we find James, aged 30 and incomplete. To his own mind, he was a distinguished intellectual, master of the best of European civilisation. Yet England he knew at second hand, through books, through her colonial system and through the life that she imposed on her subjects. England herself he had never seen. With the wider world, he was even less familiar. Neither the 1914–18 war nor the Russian Revolution had brought any response from him. 'In politics I took little interest.' Or, as James wrote elsewhere, 'Politics seemed remote from me. I was wrong and it took nearly fifty years to discover how wrong I was.'[39]

Under the influence of two charismatic figures the real C L R James at last began to emerge. The first was Captain André Cipriani, the mayor of Port of Spain and an early advocate of self-government for the West Indies. James was a government servant, banned by law from taking any part in politics. Yet life itself taught him the injustice of colonial rule, under which black could never govern white. Cipriani was a lawyer, and a former cricketer, who in 1913 had been part of the Trinidad side that scored 334 in one innings against the MCC.[40] Cipriani later led Trinidadian soldiers in the war. In James' account, the speed with which the soldiers 'adjusted themselves to the spiritual and material requirements of a modern war amazed all observers, from [General] Allenby down. Cipriani made a reputation for himself by his militant defence of the regiment against all prejudice, official and unofficial. To the end of his days he spoke constantly of the recognition they had won'. Cipriani returned to the island in 1919, becoming a leading figure in the Trinidad Workingmen's Association, and supporting the dock strikes that closed Port of Spain in the same year. In 1922, Cipriani established a publication *The Socialist* campaigning for shorter working hours. Cipriani was elected to the Trinidad legislative assembly. James began to read his magazine soon after.[41] James knew Cipriani and considered writing for his magazine.

In Trinidad, James also began to take stock of the papers of the black liberation movement, including Marcus Garvey's *The Negro World* and W E B DuBois' *The Crisis*. Du Bois was a long-standing advocate of black struggle, and later a prominent black advocate of Communism. Garvey was the founder of the Back to Africa movement, which in the immediate post-1918 period had signed up more than a million supporters. Garvey visited Port of Spain, and James later recalled travelling by train to hear him speak. Inch by inch, James was being won to the struggle for reform. He began to write a biography of Cipriani.[42] The writing of the book was intended as a means to break out of the purely contemplative radicalism into which he felt he had slipped; James wanted to employ the skills he had developed as a writer in the service of the nascent reform movement. Later, in 1932, the biography of Cipriani would be his first published book.

The second sustained influence on James was Learie Constantine, who played for Shannon against James' team Maple, and who had studied at St Anne's Government School under James' father Robert. Constantine was the very model of the professional cricketer that James had hoped to become. Learie's father L S Constantine had played against a touring MCC side in 1900 and 1906. Learie Constantine was then picked to play for the West Indies in 1923, when he was just 22 years old. He held his position in the team for the next 16 years. Before being chosen to play for the islands, Constantine had played just three first-class games. By 1928, he was the dominant figure within the West Indies team.

The essence of James' friendship with Learie Constantine is well expressed in James' memory of a single, but vital conversation with him. James at 30 was still an admirer of the English. There was so much they had taught him. Even physically, they struck him as better-fed, more skilled, truer athletes, than the people of the Caribbean. But the English he knew at a distance, chiefly through their schools, their political institutions and their literature. Learie Constantine, the sporting professional, had seen the English closer-to. He knew them as people. Around the time that Constantine was first chosen to play for the West Indies, James engaged him in talk, 'I was holding forth about some example of low West Indian cricket morals when Constantine grew grave with an almost aggressive expression in his face. "You have it all wrong, you know", he said coldly. "What did I have all wrong?" "You have it all wrong. You believe all that you read in those books. They are no better than we." I floundered around. I hadn't intended to say that they were better than we. Yet a great deal of what I had been saying was just that.' Forced to confront his deepest feelings, this was one of those charged conversations that would stay with James for many years.[43]

Tours of England gave Constantine a new profile. In later years, James would take pride in recounting some of the statistics of his friend's success. Playing in England in 1928, Constantine scored 1,381 runs at an average of 34.5 and took 107 wickets at a cost of just 22.9. The rules of judging an all-rounder's career are simple. If the average number of runs they score per innings (when batting) is higher than the average number of runs that they concede per wicket (when bowling), then they justify a place in their teams. Former England all-rounder Ian Botham finished with Test averages of 33.3 as a batsman and 28.4 as a bowler, while as I write current England all-rounder Andrew 'Freddie' Flintoff has Test averages of 32.6 and 32.8.[44] If an all-rounder's batting average is ten runs higher than their bowling average, then like Constantine in 1928 they are exceptional.

As Constantine settled in Lancashire, 'a new and inexhaustible topic, England and the English people', was added to James' discussions with his friend. By the early 1930s, Constantine was planning to write an auto-biographical history of West Indian cricket. He invited James to help him. The decision to leave marked the end of James' marriage to Juanita: 'There was some sort of arrangement whereby she was to come to meet me in England, but she saw after a time that I did not really need her and her pride rebelled.' James left Trinidad in 1932. He took with him the draft of a novel about life in the shantytowns of Port of Spain, and the draft also of his biography of Cipriani. 'The British intellectual,' he wrote, 'was going to Britain.'[45] James would not return home for more than two decades.

2

Nelson

(Previous page) Learie Nicholas Constantine (1901–71).

Arriving at Plymouth in the Spring of 1932, James made his way indirectly to the town of Nelson in Lancashire. He lived briefly just south of Euston station. Through the editors of the magazines that had published his short stories, he was able to acquire a ticket to the British Library and he was able to break into the fringes of Bloomsbury literary life. He was invited to attend a lecture given by Edith Sitwell at the Student Movement House. Sitwell read from her own poems and made a number of pronouncements on the state of world literature. She declared D H Lawrence to be 'hot' and 'woolly', and described an American novelist aged 32 who would soon have outpaced Lawrence. No one could draw the name of this writer. James realised, immediately, that she must have been referring to William Faulkner. He declared the name to Sitwell after, and she admitted that he was correct. The anecdote conveys the proximity between speaker and audience. 'That is Bloomsbury. Some group or society is always having lectures or talks by some distinguished person who comes and talks and is always willing to do anything for anyone who wishes assistance or guidance of some sort.'[46]

James enjoyed London student life and wrote glowing accounts of the range of cultural activities open to anyone who lived in the city. He also noticed that London women seemed more independent than their counterparts back home. In other respects, however, he was dissatisfied. After ten weeks in London, C L R James bought a ticket to travel north. Meeting up with Constantine, he accepted an invitation to share the family home, with Learie, his wife Norma and their daughter Gloria. James was soon busy helping to write Constantine's book, published in 1933 as *Cricket and I*. In Nelson, as well as writing, James also tried his hand at cricket. He appeared at least twice for town sides. In June 1932, for Nelson Second XI against Todmorden, James was out without scoring, but took two wickets in seven overs for just 16 runs. The following match was a friendly for the first team against Radcliffe Cricket Club. He scored six runs and took 1 for 35. This performance was not however enough to secure further games.[47]

While James' cricketing career was reaching its natural end, his friend's prospered. Between 1929 and 1937, Constantine held down a position in the Lancashire League as the Nelson club professional. 'The Nelson ground is,' James wrote, 'as pretty a ground as you could see anywhere. I had imagined a small piece of grass, fighting for its life against the gradual encroaching of cotton factories, menacing with black smoke, machine shops and tenement houses. The ground is nothing of the kind. It is full-size, level, and when you sit on the pavilion, you see on three sides a hill rising gradually covered with a green grass, clumps of trees, houses here and there, beautiful as it seems only the English countryside can be beautiful.'[48]

Nelson was then the best-supported league side in England, regularly breaking all records for gate receipts. Constantine was their star player: their most destructive bowler, their most effective batsman. Constantine's team won the league championship on seven of the nine occasions in which he played for them. Constantine's salary was £500 per year plus expenses, including return travel to Trinidad for himself and his wife plus 'third class return railways fares and a tea in all matches in which he plays for the Club away from Nelson.'* In today's prices, Constantine was paid around £80,000.

Constantine's greatness as a cricketer, James insisted, was expressed above all in his skill in fielding. The point was deliberately paradoxical. Batsman and bowlers are the usual stars. Yet James liked to tell the story of a match in 1930, between Trinidad and the MCC. The English batsman Patsy Hendren was on 98 and nervous to secure his century. The bowler Achong was holding the ball just outside the off stump, not near enough to the bat so as to force a stroke, but neither so far away as to enable the batsman to score a boundary. James used the present tense to describe what followed: 'Constantine notices that Hendren, before getting down to face Achong once more, takes a quick glance at the wide spaces between gully and second slip. Achong bowls the same balls as before. Hendren cuts to pierce the gap he has spotted between

---

* A copy of Constantine's contract is on display at the Nalis museum in Trinidad.

Constantine at gully and second slip, only to see that Constantine has anticipated the stroke and is making what is apparently an easy catch from not a bad but an ill-judged stroke.'[49]

As the best-known West Indian in the country, Constantine was frequently invited to address meetings of trade unions, employers' or professional associations. To save himself the burden, Constantine developed a regular working arrangement. Invited to speak, he would appear but utter just a few sentences. James would follow, entertaining and instructing the audiences as required. In doing this work, James gave Learie a chance to rest, often after a tiring day in the field. He released Constantine, who was expected in his sporting life to be a friend of mill owners and mill workers alike, from having to adjudicate in Nelson's internal disputes. Perhaps most of all, James saved Constantine from having to explain to each audience anew the simple facts of colour, for there were few other black families in Lancashire at this time, and prejudice, innocent or intended, was a regular companion. Years later, Constantine would tell the story of 'a little white boy whose parents were old friends of mine'. 'Soon the little fellow started school. On his very first day he ran back steaming with tears and crying out at me in broken-hearted reproach, "Uncle Learie, you never told me you were coloured!" They had given him a bad time, these other little boys and girls, when they discovered he had a friend with a different coloured skin.'[50]

It may seem strange that Constantine's celebrity could be made not just by playing Test cricket (the most prestigious layer of the game), and not in county cricket (the second layer, from which Test players were usually chosen), but in the third layer: league cricket. To explain this conundrum we must start with a sense of the enormous appeal that cricket had in the 1930s. 'In so far as cricket was played and followed throughout the country by all social classes and by both men and women', writes Ross McKibbin, 'it was the most "national" of all sports. It was administered by the upper and upper middle classes, was the predominant sport in both independent and grammar schools, and was, even more than rugby, a socially useful sport which men did not hesitate to use for the advancement of their careers; but the majority of professional cricketers were of working-class origin and, although never as important to working men as football, nor played by as many, cricket was closely followed by them, particularly by skilled working men.'[51]

There were many differences between county and league cricket. The former was and is played during the week. The matches lasted three days. Because few people had the opportunity to take three successive days off work, inevitably the crowds were smaller and were confined largely to the propertied. League cricket, by contrast, was played at weekends. It was a one-day game, and the audience for it was large, boisterous and proletarian. In contrast to the idea of cricket as a sport played by amateurs for the game's own sake, the local leagues were hard-fought, commercial affairs. An urban myth held that wicket-keepers in the Yorkshire League would play with a pin sticking in front of one of their boots to nudge of the bails if the ball came close to the stumps.[52]

James was familiar with the racial boundaries of cricket in Trinidad. In England, he learned that class hierarchies could be equally rigid. The social history of English Test and county cricket in this period is dominated by the divide between amateurs and professionals. Amateurs, ostensibly, worked in the game with no other significant means of support. In the same way that the captaincy of the West Indies cricket team was restricted to a white player, so the captaincy of the English cricket team was restricted to amateurs. Lord Hawke declared in 1925, 'Pray God no professional may ever captain England.' In 1934, when the MCC played Australia only one professional was chosen for the MCC, Patsy Hendren. But the division between amateur and professional always displayed a smell of hypocrisy. The celebrated Nottingham fast bowler Harold Larwood declared in his memoirs, reflecting on his rivalry with the Australian batsman Donald Bradman, 'I couldn't help but thinking how Fate had treated us both. Don was on the [Australian] Board of Cricket Control. I was working for a living on the assembly line of a soft drink firm. *And Don was the amateur.*'[53] The Lancashire League escaped a good deal of cant by limiting all sides to just one professional.

They were typically the stars of each side. They were assumed to be the best (and were always best-paid) of all the players.

The two counties in which cricket enjoyed a mass, working-class audience were Yorkshire and Lancashire. Of the 21 inter-war county championships, Yorkshire won twelve and Lancashire five. But Yorkshire's success at that level was not matched in the tier below. Of the local leagues, Lancashire's had the highest standard of cricket. Of all the Lancashire League teams, Nelson was the most successful. Constantine was not the first international celebrity to sign for Nelson. In 1922, Nelson employed Australian fast bowler Ted McDonald for the then unprecedented sum of £700 per year. To give an indication of the league's status, in August 1931 another Lancashire side, Accrington, came within an ace of signing Don Bradman, the most prolific batsman of that or any other era.

Although his time in Nelson was to play a key role in shaping first James's idea of Britain, and then his entire view of the world, James wrote little about the town. We are forced to rely on other sources to provide context. Nelson was a cotton town. In the 1920s, the town's unemployment rate had been modest, and lower than the national average of 6 per cent. The politics of Nelson were generally those of the left, often the far left. Such parties as the Social Democratic Federation, the Independent Labour Party, the Labour Party and the trade unions had all enjoyed a base in the area, often for several decades. In the 1929 election, Labour's Arthur Greenwood was elected as the town's MP.

Weaving suffered badly after the 1929 Wall Street Crash. Many small firms were forced out of existence, and where businesses did keep going, they did so with a reduced workforce. We should not exaggerate. The Depression was a significant blow to Nelson's prosperity, but unlike Jarrow in the North East the town was not murdered. The Nelson manufacturers specialised in producing high-quality cloth, sold in England or exported to Canada or Australia. The weavers of neighbouring Oldham and Burnley, producing medium-quality cloth, were more vulnerable to competition from overseas. Nelson's unemployment stood at an alarming

25 per cent in 1931, but fell thereafter to 18 per cent in 1932 and 12 per cent in 1936 and 1937. In Burnley, by contrast, up to 33 per cent of the population was unemployed, and the number of people out of work was to remain higher than in Nelson through the decade. By 1930, however, as a result of the industrial recession, Nelson's politics were in flux, with Labour's hegemony being challenged both on the left and the right. Rival candidates did enough to weaken Labour, but were not strong enough to win on their own. In 1931, as a result, at the peak of the town's misery, the workers of Nelson threw out their Labour MP and replaced him with the bowler-hatted, cigar-smoking Tory, Linton Thorp. By 1935, however, Thorp's majority of nearly 8,000 had been reversed, and the town was back in Labour hands, where it would remain.

We can place James' arrival in Nelson, then, at an exact stage in the local electoral cycle: poverty was omnipresent, but confidence was slowly returning and workers were turning to the left. Industrial employment and party loyalty shaped workers' conception of Britain's place in the world. Throughout Lancashire, cotton was already a globalised industry, with production for export through the Empire, and prosperity chal-lenged by the threat of rival importers. Many of the workers were better educated in colonial politics than their bosses. Gandhi had visited the mill towns of Lancashire and been warmly received. James was address-ing an audience that identified with the Labour Party, and expected it to deliver on the long promise of colonial freedom.[54]

There is one contemporary source in which James reflected on his expe-riences of the town. Shortly after arriving in Nelson, he sent a letter back from England explaining his preference for his new home over London: it began with a conflict between the owners of the town's cinemas and the people who worked for them. 'In Nelson,' James explained, 'a few years ago there were three or four talking-picture houses run by men who were strangers to the town. The Nelson people are very fond of the cinema. They flock to it in their thousands. For many, apart from the beauties of nature, an abiding love of the English people, the cinema is the only recreation.' The Nelson operators were paid at this time around

45 shillings a week, and the owners of the theatres decided to reduce their salaries.' What followed was a boycott by the town's public, who refused to consent to any lowering of pay.* James concluded: 'It was magnificent and it was war. I confess I was thrilled to the bone when I heard it. I could forgive England all the vulgarity and all the depressing disappointment of London for the magnificent spirit of these north country working people. As long as that is the spirit of which they are made, then indeed Britons never, never shall be slaves.'[55]

Seventy years later, it is hard to know how much of this story is true. There are no records of the cinemagoers' stay-away in Nelson Library, nor in the region's centre for socialist history, the Salford Working-Class Movement Library. Neither has the dispute been recorded in the pages of the journal *North West Labour History*.[56] Those who worked in the industry in later years recall that cinemas were rated from AA through B to C. The AA category applied to large cinemas like the Odeon in London's Leicester Square, the C to relative fleapits. The rating then governed the pay scale of the projectionists. It is possible that a strike

---

* 'Nelson is a town where most of the working people are pretty closely united. So, in order to avoid trouble, the owners who ran cinemas in Burnley, a much bigger town a few miles away, hit on an ingenious plan of attaining their ends. They reduced salaries in Burnley. They attempted to transfer a Nelson operator to a Burnley theatre. Naturally the pay would be the Burnley pay, and thus the salaries would be lowered. Note, please, how careful the owners had to be in such a simple matter of lowering the salary of an ordinary cinema machine operator ... The Nelson people got wind of the matter. There were meetings and discussions. They decided that the salaries of the cinema operators should not be lowered. Complications began. The owners insisted. One cannot be certain of the details. But what matters is that the whole town of Nelson, so to speak, went on strike. They would not go to the cinema. The pickets were put out in order to turn back those who tried to go. For days the cinemas played to empty benches. In a town of forty thousand people you could find sometimes no more than half a dozen in the theatres. The company went bankrupt and had to leave. Whereupon local people took over and the theatres again began to be filled. C L R James, 'The Nucleus of a Great Civilisation', *Port of Spain Gazette* (28 August 1932).

of projectionists or a consumer boycott might have been triggered by the owners altering the rating of the cinemas in order to lower wages and while they might have succeeded with this in moderate Burnley, there could easily have been a different response in the militant town of Nelson. We should note that James prefaced the story with the phrase 'a few years ago'. His language was so vague, that it is almost as if he doubted his own veracity. Alternatively, it is possible that the story should be read differently, as a statement of what people in the town would have liked to have done, or really 'should' have done in light of their local reputation. For the year of James' arrival also witnessed the well-documented More Looms Dispute of the Nelson weavers.

In early 1932, employers in a majority of factories in neighbouring Blackburn and Burnley, but not Nelson, terminated agreements with the weavers' union. The workers responded by balloting, with 16,618 voting for a strike and just 1,908 against, but strike action was postponed. In many factories, employers saw the danger, and returned to previous rates, but not all. There was a strike at Shuttleworth's Mill, during which the police used batons to attack picketing workers. In April, employers came back with a demand for a one-sixth cut in wages. A strike began in earnest on 24 July, just four weeks before James' article was printed in Trinidad. At first, the union allowed workers to strike only in Burnley (was this moment the source, in James' anecdote, of the tensions between the two towns?). In Nelson, it will be recalled, the recession had been shallower. Workers were more confident, and the employers more nervous. The weavers' federation, wary of a prolonged dispute, instructed its members in Nelson not to strike. They in turn were incensed. Soon Nelson was in the hands of the unions. A number of leading Communists could be seen leading the crowd: Robin Page Arnot, a veteran of the 1926 general strike, James Rushton, a local weaver who had been sent for training in Moscow, Rose Smith, a founding member of the party and of the workers' Minority Movement, and the former Communist MP for Battersea, Shapurji Saklatvala.

At the start of September, the union agreed to a Lancashire-wide strike: in effect, to include Nelson as well as Burnley. Unions raised £12,000 in donations to support the strike. The strike ended at the end of the month with agreement between the owners and the union: a pay cut was accepted, although far less than the employers had intended, and with a promise of no victimisation. It was a compromise, but no victory. The Nelson weavers debated the agreement in September at a meeting in the town's Imperial ballroom (the Palace cinema was used for an overflow meeting). The workers refused to go back, and even discussed leaving the union, but were persuaded to remain by a further series of agreements, which included full recognition of the union. It is hard to think of a town in Britain that was more radical at this time.[57]

In Nelson, James was busy reading. He came to see some of the limitations of his own former views. Prior to his arrival in Nelson, his schooling, his cricketing career and the movement in Trinidad for colonial reform had been the forces that had had the most impact upon him. In British terms, these influences were compatible with a range of politics, from a moderate Conservatism to a moderate or radical Liberalism. The impact of his schooling, of course, continued to be felt. Yet James was changing. He became a different person in England. 'I was a Labour Party man,' he later reported, 'but I found myself to the left of the Labour Party in Nelson, militant as that was.' Or, as he wrote elsewhere: 'My labour and socialist ideas had been got from books and were rather abstract. These cynical working men were a revelation and brought me down to earth.'[58] James was inching towards a wider conception of life, one that would take in philosophy and even revolution.

After 1932, James wrote: 'Fiction-writing drained out of me and was replaced by politics.' To understand James' openness to this turn, we should return briefly to 'Revolution', the last story that he wrote before leaving Trinidad. At the heart of the story is a failed insurrection: 'There weren't many, no more than a hundred or so, but if they had landed and taken the city and shown they had guns, they would have had a big following at once. All the people would have been with them. All the people are with us. They are against [the dictator] Gómez. But the

Venezuelan is not going to leave his cattle and his wife and children any more until he sees something is happening. For too many years the revolutionary party in Venezuela has been fooling the people.'[59] The lessons are simple: the people are ready to revolt, they only lack leaders. A way must be found to restore the revolution to the purity of its goals. Brief as this passage is, and belonging to an earlier period in James' development, it stands as a summary for the politics that he would choose. The ideas were already in him; in Nelson, they had the chance to develop.

In 1932, James published *The Life of Captain Cipriani: An Account of British Government in the West Indies*, his first book. It combines a biography of Cipriani with polemical chapters arguing for West Indian home rule. 'When will British administrators learn the lesson,' James wrote, 'and for the sake of future cordial relations give willingly and cheerfully what they know they will have to give at last? How do they serve their posterity by leaving them a heritage of bitterness and hate in every quarter of the globe?' James' title was modest. 'Self-government' means autonomy, rather than necessarily independence. His message was still one of reform. Constantine helped to pay for the printing. The book secured few reviews, but was noticed by an old Bloomsbury contact Leonard Woolf, who invited James to re-publish the later chapters as a further pamphlet, *The Case for West Indian Self-Government*.[60]

The Life of Captain Cipriani was soon followed by Constantine's book, *Cricket and I*. The latter was dedicated 'to my West Indian friend C L R James who has given me valuable assistance in writing this book'. *Cricket and I* described what it meant to be the Nelson professional. It was a format in which batsmen would play in an unorthodox fashion, and bowlers needed to think harder than they might even in Test cricket. 'A great success in county cricket and even moderate success in Test cricket does not qualify a man for success in league cricket.' As the team went into bat, the professional should wait and see if the opposing team had a star bowler. His role then would be to bat his antagonist out of the attack. 'Above all', the professional 'should not let the great man on the opposite side get him out.' 'Sometimes the professional has to bat at both ends in

order to help a young player round a difficult corner.' Sometimes, he had
to bat cautiously, to preserve his wicket. When bowling, the tactics were
reversed: to wait for other team's star and to prise him out. There were
often rewards in caution. The other trick was to bring a sense of theatre
to the performance. 'Atmosphere counts in every class of cricket, but
particularly in league cricket, and he who can create it is far on the road
to success.' Lastly, the book insisted, the contribution of the professional
could only be measured through his team's collective success, 'I am not
preaching here any gospel of true sportsmanship. If even the professional
is the essence of selfishness, and thinks only of doing well for himself, it
will pay him in the end to study and help his side as much as possible;
for it is with them that he has to play and no man can consistently beat
eleven others at cricket.'[61] It is impossible to know the extent to which
such passages represented merely Learie Constantine talking, or how
far they were strained through his friend's intellect. What we do know,
however, is that James reflected long on Constantine's words. Thirty
years later, his analysis of Constantine's method would stand right at the
heart of James' *Beyond a Boundary*, his defining work.

3

London

(Previous page) The Australian batsman Woodfull ducking a bumper from England bowler Harold Larwood in the Test Series in Australia controversial for 'Bodyline' bowling.

In the midst of all this writing, James was also busy reading. If he is to be believed then the decisive push towards his adoption of new ideas came from studying two substantial books, Oswald Spengler's *Decline of the West* and Leon Trotsky's *History of the Russian Revolution*. 'What Spengler did for me was to discover the pattern and development of different types of society. It took me away from the individual and the battles and concerns with the kinds of things that I had learned in conventional history. Trotsky did this also by his reference to historical development.'[62]

Of the two books, the first is the more surprising influence. Oswald Spengler argued that all civilisations had a limited duration, comparable to the cycles of organic life. All cultures reach a phase of 'Civilisation', a period of senescence characterised by the rise of large cities, and their domination by corrupt politicians. Spengler held that Europe was in inevitable decline. There had been no literary innovation in Europe since the 1770s, no musical progress since Wagner. Yet just at the moment when Europe seemed doomed to annihilation, her prospects were not fixed. A new flurry of energy was still possible. In Spengler's account, 'Now dawns the time when the form-filled powers of the blood, which the rationalism of the Megalopolis has suppressed, reawaken in the depth. Everything in the order of dynastic tradition and old nobility that has saved itself up for the future, everything that there is of high money-disdaining ethic, everything that is intrinsically sound enough to be, in Frederick the Great's words, the *servant*, the hard-working, self-sacrificing, caring *servant* of the State, all this becomes suddenly the focus of immense life-forces.'[63] A new Frederick was needed to rescue Germany and Europe from their otherwise inevitable decline. Oswald Spengler's politics were those of the German authoritarian right. In his home country, Spengler's book was part of a pessimistic intellectual culture that was on the verge of adopting fascism, but to a non-European, the message of *The Decline of the West* must have been different. If Europe was indeed in terminal decline, then what other power would supplant her? If Europe was to fall to some rival, to a Russia or an America, how could the subjects of empire free themselves?

In Trotsky, James found an answer to these questions.* The future belonged to the Russia of 1917. There were many features of Trotsky's book that impressed James, his passionate identification with the dispossessed, the author's belief that his campaign was the cause of history, Trotsky's own considerable reading and his ability to connect events in Russia with others taking place all over the world. The aspect that James recalled later was the breadth of its author's Marxist theory: 'Something happened which I found among the Marxists whom I got to know. They read the Marxist documents and then read some of the classics of European literature, fitting them into Marx's historical scheme. Not me. As I read Trotsky's book I was already familiar with all the references to history and literature that he was making. I was able automatically and without difficulty to absorb his argument and the logical line that he presented.'[64]

C L R James' self-confidence in this period and later is an endearing trait. It was often as if his very own brilliance astounded him. There may have been deeper factors as well. We can recall the humiliations suffered by the educated men of James' childhood, such as his friend Padmore's father, James Alfonso Nurse. We can reflect also on James' role as Constantine's regular mouthpiece, the man charged with representing an entire region. He was a success in this work. People were charmed by his genius. At a certain point he must have been bored by the surprise of many British audiences. One part of James' response was disdain in response to such stupidity and a rightful pride.

Yet James was not quite as widely read as he claimed. Cognisant of

---

* Leon Trotsky (1879–1940) was with Lenin one of the two leading figures of the Russian Revolution. After 1917, Trotsky was the People's Commissar for Foreign Affairs, later the founder of the Red Army and People's Commissar for War. Pushed out by the rise of Stalin in the 1920s, Trotsky was expelled from the Communist Party and deported from the Soviet Union. In exile, he was the great focal point for revolutionaries who opposed Stalin while continuing to support the original goals of 1917.

19th-century literature he certainly was, but James was still unfamiliar with the Marxist classics: he would read the first volume of *Capital* much later, as we shall see. Only through Trotsky did James begin to realise that there was a Marxist literature to master.

Trotsky's *History of the Russian Revolution* is a narrative of the events leading up to 1917. It describes the venality of the Tsarist system, the contradictions of a society that combined rapid economic growth with authoritarian rule. Trotsky records the strikes and bread riots from which the February and October revolutions were born. He gives pride of place to Lenin, who by arguing with his comrades in the Bolshevik party for the necessity of a second revolution had played the decisive part in making that revolution possible. The book ends with the Bolshevik system established, but still young and optimistic.[65] At the end of the book, Lenin is still alive and Stalin barely mentioned.

Trotsky's *History* shows the Russia of 1917 as a paragon of the most extreme democracy, the yardstick against which any other society should be judged. 'Milton says that a great book is the precious life-blood of a master-spirit. True', C L R James wrote, 'But the *History* is the precious life-blood of many master spirits; and also of the Russian people, of the French proletariat, in 1848 and 1871, of Ironsides and Jacobins and sans culottes, of the abortive German revolution of 1918, of the Chinese and other nationalist revolutions. All are there. All had contributed their sufferings, their hopes, the wisdom that was drawn from their experiences. A hundred years of socialist thought and proletarian struggles have gone into the making of that book.'[66]

The reference to China is significant. Trotsky came from the ranks of a European left. He was familiar with Berlin and Paris, but not Johannesburg or Lagos. Does this mean that his Marxism was only interested in Western revolt, or did Trotsky's consider the role played by struggle in Africa and Asia? The history of 19th-century socialism suggests that either choice was open. The best of the dissident Marxists took their cue from Marx. He was among the first Europeans to support African and Asian struggles for liberation, and backed the Chinese revolt against the

British of 1853 and the Indian uprising of 1857–9. He argued that human liberation was impossible without the emancipation of all the oppressed. Following Marx's death in 1883, it was assumed that Marxists stood for the abolition of all empires. Yet by the end of the century the socialist parties in each country had moved towards different politics. As they were successful in elections to parliament, their politics became more respectable. The attitude towards Empire changed. The bible of the socialist right was Edward Bernstein's book *Evolutionary Socialism*. Bernstein maintained that in annexing large parts of Africa, Germany was only 'carrying out its honourable share in the civilising work of the world'.[67]

The pattern of the 19th century was repeated in the 20th. After the success of the 1917 Revolution in Russia, the energy was with a younger generation of socialists who saw in the Bolshevik victory not just a general message of working-class revolt, but also the particular claim that the old Western European powers were in decline and that the colonial masses should rise against them. But over time, many reneged on this initial stance. The Communist Parties played a key role. Before Stalin's rise to power, the Western Communist Parties recruited people who instinctively championed colonial liberation struggles. Yet the longer Stalin dominated the Soviet Union, the more the Communists in every other country were expected to treat their own foreign policy as a continuation of Soviet interests. The parties of the developing world were assigned to the Communist Parties of 'their' colonial state. From the 1930s onwards, the Communist groups in Egypt had to have their policies approved by Communists in France.[68] Communists in Britain dictated instructions to Communists in India.

Naturally, this process introduced a certain cynicism into what should have been the discussions of equals. The Algerian revolutionary Frantz Fanon was shocked to discover French Communists backing the French government against the desire of Algerians for independence.[69] Even when the Western Communists did call for liberty, they tended to do so in a very mechanical fashion. Liberation was described as taking place only in distinct stages. First, a local state would emancipate itself from colonial rule, and only long after could workers' issues be raised. Under Communist leadership, even victorious struggles tended to produce a new native ruling class that was concerned only to build up its own position and cared little for the people it now ruled.

Within Trotsky there was the germ of an alternative approach. In Marx's day, and for most of his first generation of followers, it was assumed that any socialist revolution would take place first in a country like Germany or France. As the world's major economic power, Britain was unlikely to fall to revolution. Both Marx and Engels fulminated against the 'bourgeois' habits of the British working class. But socialism was a doctrine of economic plenty. Its philosophy was one of redistributing more widely the resources that had already been accumulated under capitalism. Socialism would come to Russia, it was assumed, only after it had triumphed in Britain, France or Germany. In the early passages of Trotsky's *History*, the author engages with this view. What enabled the Russian revolution, Trotsky argued, was in fact the dual and incomplete character of Russian economic growth. Russia was so poor in 1914 or 1917, that her people demanded revolution. She was so poorly developed that no socialist society could be developed in Russia alone. What was needed, Trotsky argued, was a European revolution that would enable the militant workers of Russia to combine with their more prosperous comrades in the West. In the 1930s, this strategy was known as 'permanent revolution'. Developed as a model for revolution in the poorer countries of Europe, it was also impliedly a plan for revolution in the colonial world. If struggles began say in Algeria, but spread to France; or if protests prospered in the West Indies and spread from there to Britain, then what began as a colonial revolt could spark a socialist revolution in the centre of world capitalism. In both the centre and periphery, workers could rule. This was of course a hugely ambitious theory. Its grandeur helps explain its attraction to James.

It is in this very context that C L R James' work takes on its special importance. The legacy of Stalinism could be taken to show that Marxist ideas were of no use to the victims of colonialism. In Trotsky, there was the possibility of an alternative approach, but it remained underdeveloped. Not all of this could have been obvious to James as he poured over Trotsky's book, but some of it must have been. In James, we can see the attempt to take this part of Trotsky's legacy seriously. Before James encountered Trotsky's _History_, his radicalism was passive. He rejected the existing condition of things, but had no confidence that people could change. One book later, 'I wanted to meet some Trotskyists'.[70]

James' adoption of Trotskyist politics coincided with a move to London in 1933. He was able to move because he was no longer financially dependent on Constantine. Around the time that Learie Constantine's _Cricket and I_ appeared, James found work with Neville Cardus as a cricket correspondent for the _Manchester Guardian_. His career as a sports journalist began with an article describing a match between Nelson and another local side, Rawtenstall. The piece was dedicated to the Rawtenstall bowler, S F Barnes, dubbed by James 'the greatest of all bowlers. To begin with, Barnes not only is fifty-nine, but looks it. Some cricketers at fifty-nine look and move like men in their thirties. Not so Barnes. You can almost hear the old bones creaking. He is tall and thin, well over six feet, with strong features. It is rather a remarkable face in its way, and could belong to a great lawyer or a statesman without incongruity. He holds his head well back, with the long chin rather lifted. He looks like a man who has seen as much of the world as he wants to see.' Constantine was playing for Nelson, and the contest between bowler and batsman made James' report. 'When Constantine came in I looked for a duel. Constantine was not going to be drawn into playing forward. Barnes was not going to bowl short to be hooked over the pavilion, or over-pitch to be hit into the football field. Constantine was also not going to chance it. For on that turning wicket, to such accurate bowling, who chanced it was lost.'[71]

For another piece, James witnessed a Don Bradman century at Scarborough. 'After the first excitement, this sort of thing becomes slightly monotonous. A bowler bowls, Bradman makes a stroke, not a single fieldsman moves, and the ball is returned from the boundary. The essence of any game is conflict, and there was no conflict here, the superiority on one side was too overwhelming.'[72]

A third piece, an article on the West Indian side playing at the Oval in 1933, has echoes of the debates that would shape English sporting journalism 40 and 50 years later. Was it fair that the West Indies were allowed to pick such a fast and threatening attack? 'The English were childishly helpless,' James wrote back to the *Port of Spain Gazette*, 'against the fast bowling. And it was not bodyline because there was only one man forward short leg on the side. The change bowling, however, was weak. Whether [the West Indies captain] Grant will allow himself to be frightened by these English critics is an important question. If he breaks the morale of his fast bowlers by expressing doubts as to whether the tactics of [his strike bowlers] Constantine and Martindale are fair, the West Indies should flay him alive.'[73]

James' anxieties, that English journalists and cricketing authorities would put pressure on the West Indies captain to instruct his bowlers to bowl more slowly, were justified. The senior statesman of West Indies cricket was then Sir Pelham 'Plum' Warner. He had played a positive role in previous decades, arguing that West Indian teams should contain substantial numbers of black (as well as white) cricketers, and that the matches between the West Indies and England should be granted Test status. By 1933, it will be recalled, the West Indies had held it for just five years. At the time of the 1933 tour, Warner criticised his own team's bowlers for having adopted 'body-line' tactics, commenting that one ball from Learie Constantine had missed England batsman Douglas Jardine by 'a fraction of an inch'.[74]

The phrase 'bodyline' was but a year old, having been coined to describe the tactics of Jardine's own team the previous year in Australia. Faced with the irrepressible batting of Australia's Donald Bradman, Jardine had developed two innovations. First, he instructed his bowlers, especially Harold Larwood, to bowl short balls, fast towards Bradman and other batsmen's bodies. Secondly, Jardine picked a cordon of fielders on the batsman's leg-side and backward of square leg, so that players

simply trying to protect themselves with the bat would be more likely
to offer sharp, glancing catches off their body. This dual tactic relied on
the batsman's fear of getting hurt. It was cricket by force and the threat
of violence. The tactic caused a fierce argument in Australia, where
bodyline was dubbed tantamount to cheating. The Australian Board of
Control for Cricket (ABCC) sent a cable to the MCC in London: 'Bodyline bowling ... menace[s] best interests of game, making protection
of body by batsmen the main consideration. Causing intensely bitter
feeling between players as well as injury. In our opinion is unsportsman-
like. Unless stopped at once likely to upset friendly relations existing
between Australia and England.' The ABCC was forced to back down
and the tactic continued. But on return to England, Jardine's professional
bowlers were ordered to apologise. Harold Larwood famously refused,
pointing out that he had bowled unwillingly and under orders from his
amateur captain. Larwood never played for England again, and eventually settled in Australia. In *Beyond a Boundary*, C L R James would later
describe bodyline as 'The blow from which "It isn't cricket" has never
recovered ... Bodyline was not an incident, it was not an accident, it was
not a temporary aberration. It was the violence and ferocity of our age
expressing itself in cricket.'[75]

The major concern of the English authorities, then, as their players
faced the West Indies during the 1933 series was to pretend that nothing
untoward had happened in Australia under Jardine. The concern of the
West Indian bowlers was chiefly to take English wickets. But as James
explains in the passage we have cited above, Constantine and his col-
leagues were no mugs. They bowled short and fast, but held back from
setting a bodyline field. 'There was only one man forward short leg on
the side.'[76] The concern of Warner meanwhile was to protect the long-
term status of West Indian cricket. That meant backing down.

Knowing of the controversy and the doubts within the West Indies
camp, English batsmen claimed the mantle of victimhood. 'In the MCC
game against us in May at Lord's', Learie Constantine would later recall,
one English batsman Patrick Hendren, 'came to bat in this thing, a

cricket cap specially padded with thick rubber, and with the peaks of two other caps coming down to guard temple and ears. Patsy put on this garment only when I bowled. The effectiveness of the shield remained doubtful as he never headed even one ... Incidentally, [the West Indian batsman] George Headley was knocked out for more than five minutes by a leg-side bumper during that innings, and others of us took some hard knocks. We discussed the possibility of asking Patsy to lend us his helmet, but did not do so from fear of starting something which, with press sensitivities to bodyline maters at that time, might have had a bad effect ... Headley missed the next three matches.'[77]

In accusing the West Indians of playing bodyline cricket, the English cricketing authorities were exaggerating to hide their own previous culpability (against Australia), and for other reasons as well. At the risk of anachronism, it is only right to quote an argument that Chris Searle would make several decades later, at a time when supporters of West Indian cricket did not share the circumspection of Warner (or even James) in 1933: 'There is no doubt that for some English and American cricket "experts", sunk into the conservative traditions of the sport, the prospect of an exceptionally fast Caribbean man with a cricket ball carries the same threat as a rebellious, anti-imperial black man with a gun. They want him suppressed, disarmed, he fits nowhere into their rules and ways of the game and only challenges them.'[78] Those of us who can recall vividly the West Indies cricket tours of England in the 1980s, and in particular the response of the press to a talented generation of Caribbean bowlers, will recognise the truth of Searle's analysis.

The England team was vulnerable, James insisted, the West Indies lacked only self-belief. 'West Indians are among the most highly gifted people one can find anywhere. The English have money, thirty times our population, vast organization, every conceivable advantage. Yet with all that, we could hold our own. Our trouble is that we have not yet learned to subordinate everything to winning. Under modern conditions to win you have to make up your mind to win. The day West Indians White Brown and Black learn to be West Indians, to see nothing in front to right or left but West Indian success and the means to it, the day they begin to grow up. Along with that it will be necessary to cultivate any number of fine speeches, noble sentiments and unimpeachable principles. But these you must indulge in before the struggle, cricket or whatever it may be, and also after the struggle is over.'[79] As James was becoming more confident and independent in his politics, so his views on the ethical content of cricket were changing. He was less willing to see the rules as a neutral terrain. He was better attuned to the habits of patronage or dishonesty from those who had the most power within the game. He was starting to see cricket as a location not of peace but of war.

Cricket and politics were intermixed. To support the West Indies team was implicitly to call for self-government. Change in the Caribbean required change in England too. It was in London that James identified himself for the first time as a revolutionary. 'I joined the Labour Party in London and there I met the Trotskyists who were distributing a pamphlet. The Trotskyists decided to go into the ILP [the Independent Labour Party] and I went with them'. James was living in Hampstead, and was soon speaking for his comrades at meetings there and at Speakers' Corner. He was also active in campaigns for colonial freedom, 'so I would speak for the Trotskyist movement and then walk about a hundred yards to where the black movement was speaking. There was always a lot of comic laughter about that with which I was well acquainted.' His allies included a 'very tall, handsome', young worker called Arthur Ballard. James also met the Irish Trotskyist Nora Connolly O'Brien, 'Coming from the railway station, we crossed the river by Parliament, and she said, "You should have done away with that years ago, it is easy from the river" ... She instinctively saw the revolutionary possibilities.' Compared to O'Brien, 'the British Trotskyite revolutionaries were no more than left-wing Labour.'[80]

James' comrades were then a tiny faction, with a membership of a few dozen. They attempted to win allies within a larger party, the Independent Labour Party. The politics of the ILP were also in transition. Founded in 1893, the ILP had promoted an idea of parliamentary socialism and it was with ILP backing that the first Labour MPs, including Keir Hardie, were elected. Prior to 1918, the only way in which an individual could be a member of the Labour Party was through membership of an affiliated society, of which the ILP was the largest. After 1918, individual membership of the Labour Party was allowed, and so the ILP returned to something like its original role, as a socialist ginger group, debating ideas, generally to the left of the Labour leadership. Through the 1920s, the ILP was slowly marginalised as the Labour Party in parliament moved right under Ramsay MacDonald. Then, in 1931, MacDonald formed a National Government with the Conservatives. Everything changed. Overnight MacDonald was judged a traitor. Not just MacDonald himself, but MacDonald's politics of slow reformism were judged to be at fault. The ILP voted to quit the Labour Party and set out on its own. For the next decade, the Independent Labour Party would continue to exist as a sort of half-way house between the revolutionary ardour of the Trotskyists and the reformism of the Labour Party. By 1935, James was chair of the Finchley branch of the ILP.

Another activist, Ajit Roy, has described working with James and other Trotskyists in this period, 'Our main task was to bring out [a newspaper] *Fight* and to make open propaganda in street corner meetings. We built a portable platform and the three of us, James, a tall West Indian, Stanton, a very Jewish-looking chap from the East End, and myself, an Indian, taking the portable platform to the shopping centres all over London, regarding ourselves as the vanguard of the British proletariat! It is all very amusing – but people did listen – probably the very strangeness of it gave us an audience. But once James started speaking he always got a crowd.'[81] Not everyone was so taken with James. Another veteran socialist Ethel Mannin published *Comrade O Comrade,* a satirical account of the personalities active on the British left. One scene features a barely fictionalised 'extremely handsome young Negro' Trotskyist, who is invited to tea with the central characters Larry and Mary. By way of conversation, the Trotskyist makes a series of mini-speeches 'Blum ... Daladier ... Popular Front ... French workers ... Stalinist bureaucracy'.

'The Trotskyists arrived punctually at four and they left punctually at five', the narrator complains, 'and in that time Mary [Mannin's heroine] uttered exactly twelve words.'[82]

As C L R James immersed himself in the socialist movement, so too he played a more prominent part in the struggle for colonial freedom. Old friendships were put to new purposes. In 1933, James saw a poster for a meeting on colonial freedom, at which one of the billed speakers was a 'George Padmore – Communist.' He decided to investigate. 'The news came through that George Padmore had been expelled from the United States and had come to England. Everyone was talking about George Padmore and there was a meeting.' To James' amazement, 'Padmore' turned out to be his childhood friend, Malcolm Nurse. 'That night when we left the meeting we went to eat and finally parted at four o'clock in the morning.' Yet the 1933 meeting seemed to leave no trace; Padmore left England soon after, he and James lost contact.

Since James' departure for England, Padmore had been active in the Trinidad labour movement, taken part in the meetings of the Communist International, and met Stalin. When he found James in 1933, he was still a loyal Communist. But shortly afterwards, he became disenchanted. When the Soviet Union began seeking international alliances against Hitler, the Russian leaders instructed the Western Communists to adopt a new strategy, known by 1935 as the 'Popular Front'. At its heart was the idea that Communists should no longer seek a revolution at home, or internationally, but should form alliances with labour and liberal parties, or any group, right up to the very edges of fascism. From this new line the International chose to downplay its previous emphasis on the break-up of empires. The politics of colonial liberation no longer fitted with this policy.

Padmore chose to continue his support for African liberation. Breaking with the Communists, he took with him a number of contacts made in previous campaigns. He returned to London in 1935, renewing his friendship with C L R James. With various allies, James helped to launch first a campaign, the International African Friends of Ethiopia, and then in 1937 an International African Service Bureau. Other active supporters of these campaigns included Jomo Kenyatta, Ras Makonnen, W E F Ward and Fritz Braithwhaite. Membership was restricted to those of African descent. The Bureau needed a publication and a journal, *International African Opinion*, was launched with James its editor. This project developed from hostility to the Italian genocide in Ethiopia to opposition against the entire imperialist domination of the world. 'No-one was talking about it,' C L R James would later recall, 'and to my astonishment within thirty years there were forty new African states ... That is one of the greatest experiences of my life.'[83]

One of the most successful Trotskyist campaigns was conducted in 1935 and 1936 at the time of the Italian invasion of Abyssinia (today Ethiopia). James spoke up and down the country. His message was that the League of Nations would take no effective action to stop the war. To protest, workers should conduct their own policy of sanctions against Italy. At the time of the war, the leaders of the ILP adopted a line of support for Abyssinia. James was invited to contribute articles to the ILP paper, the *New Leader*, in which he argued against Britain's modest plans for 'peace', between Italy and Ethiopia, a peace very much on Italian terms. The deal was as dishonest, James argued, as the propaganda that had taken Britain into the last war. '"Gallant little Belgium" was bad enough, but "the independence of Ethiopia" is worse. It is the greatest swindle in all the living history of Imperialism. The British government, having mobilised world opinion and many of its own workers behind it, has put a stranglehold on Ethiopia, as tight as anything Italian Imperialism ever attempted.[84]

At the next ILP conference some of the tensions in the leadership became apparent. One party leader, Fenner Brockway, argued like James for Italy's defeat, but other long-standing leaders of the party including James Maxton began to argue something different. Their argument was that war should be resisted along pacifist lines. What would James argue, they might say, if Mussolini or Hitler took their aggression to other countries? Should a policy of workers' sanctions lead then to support for another terrible war between the Great Powers? Maxton threatened to resign over the issue. Brockway took James aside, and persuaded him not put a motion to the ILP conference criticising the leadership; he also persuaded the organisers, however, to allow a statement from James to be published. It was James' 'first experience of big politics'.[85]

James attempted a synthesis of Pan-Africanism and Trotskyism. At the time of his conversion to Marxism, James considered the two trends to be synonymous. He was not the only person to see the links. Through Padmore, James came to know members of the coming generation of African leaders, including Kwame Nkrumah. 'When I hear people arguing about Marxism versus the nationalist or racialist struggle, I am very confused. In England I edited the Trotskyist paper and I edited the nationalist, pro-African paper of George Padmore, and nobody quarrelled. The Trotskyists read and sold the African paper and ... there were African nationalists who read and sold the Trotskyist paper. I moved among them, we attended each other's meetings and there was no problem because we had the same aim in general, freedom by revolution.'[86]

Under James' influence, the British Trotskyists followed the success of the movements for colonial independence, recording in their papers the struggles in Kenya, Egypt, India, Palestine and elsewhere. Their sympathy was only a small part of an international trend towards alliance between colonial movements and radicals in the Western cities. So when he suggests that there was no contradiction between these two schools of thought, C L R James is correct for this, early, stage of the movement.

4

When Slaves Rebelled

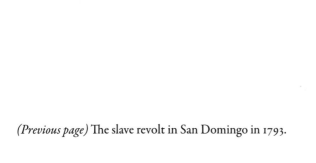

(Previous page) The slave revolt in San Domingo in 1793.

C L R James' espousal of revolution was expressed for the first time in literature when in March 1936, he oversaw the production of a play *Toussaint L'Ouverture*, based on the story of the Haitian revolts against slavery and their leader Toussaint. The play was performed at the Westminster Theatre in central London, with Paul Robeson,* the black American athlete, activist and singer, playing the title role. James' collaboration with Robeson might appear surprising, for James supported Trotsky and Robeson Stalin. But their mutual regard and desire for collaboration went much deeper. Both had long been fascinated by the story of the slave revolts. At school, Robeson had topped a state-wide debating contest with a speech in praise of Toussaint.[87] Both James and Robeson had also campaigned tirelessly against Mussolini's war. James also seems to have been captivated by Robeson's physical presence. The Trinidadian had been raised in a colonial society where white men were taller, fitter and monopolised all images of male beauty. But Robeson was an extraordinary athlete, a man who could have made his career in American football had he wished, preferring to train as a lawyer and then work as an actor and singer. We can recall Constantine's words to James years previously, 'They are no better than we.' The encounter with

---

* Paul Robeson (1898–1976) was born in New Jersey, the fifth and youngest child of Rev. William D Robeson, a former slave. He entered Rutgers College in 1915 as only the third African-American student in that institution, representing the school in baseball, basketball and football. After Rutgers, Robeson studied at Columbia law school and worked briefly as a law clerk on Wall Street. He later became a world-famous actor, celebrated for playing the part of Othello, and a singer, in which role he was feted in New York, Vienna, Prague, Budapest, Germany, Paris, Holland, London, Moscow and Nairobi. He was closely allied with the American Communist Party. He performed in eleven Hollywood films, and was best known for his role in the musical *Showboat*, singing 'Old Man River'. From the late 1940s onwards, Robeson refused to sing to audiences that were racially segregated. His concerts were often broken up by racists, however, and in the period of McCarthyism his voice was almost silenced. Between 1947 and 1958 was not even allowed to carry an American passport.

Robeson may have helped to free James.[88] Certainly, their relationship was reflected in the text, with his ally Jean-Jacques Dessalines warning Toussaint of the dangers of reliance on revolutionary France, 'You are too soft with these people. You will pay for it one day. Land for plantations – and slaves to work. That is their word, that is their God, that is their education, that is their religion. Don't trust the French. Don't trust the English. Don't trust the Americans.'[89]

James' next published work was a novel, *Minty Alley*, his most substantial work of fiction. Perhaps because it was largely written prior to his departure from Trinidad, the book is very different from the other works he published at this time. Above all, it makes no direct mention of colonial politics. Empire provides merely an assumed backdrop. There are no English characters, no civil servants, and no trace of the state. The interest of the novel lies in the characters of Mr Haynes and his landlady Mrs Rouse, the boarders and the lovers who share their lives, the people of 'the yard'. The hero of the book is a member of the downward-falling petty bourgeoisie. Although attracted to the world of the urban poor, he is still definitely outside it. An educated man, a bookstore clerk, Haynes reads, listens in hallways, meets his neighbours, and is slowly transformed by them. As well as taking the rent, Mrs Rouse is a professional cook. Her boyfriend Benoit is an occasional labourer and regular philanderer. Rouse removes her assistant Philomen in the hope of securing Benoit's sole attention. But still her suspicions continue. Benoit flees. Mrs Rouse's niece Maisie begins a dalliance with Haynes, before realising his essential passivity, in face of the old barriers of class. She too leaves. At the end of the book, the house has been sold to new owners. Haynes departs 'thinking of old times'.

Minty Alley was praised at the time for its urban realism, but what strikes now is rather the continuing distance it suggests between James (or rather, his protagonist Haynes) and the Trinidadian poor. The tone of the book is ironic, reflecting the narrator's ignorance of this plebeian world. British readers would do well to imagine the George Bowling of Orwell's *Coming Up for Air*, transplanted to the Caribbean, optimistic rather than downbeat, but compelled in the same way to maintain a precarious social standing. The story of the book is of Haynes' conversion from onlooker to participant in the lives of his poorer neighbours. All vitality is in the yard. The workers of the Caribbean need the skills of the educated. Haynes provides advice on the law and accountancy. The educated lack the vitality of the poor. Haynes is unprepared for the physicality of life. His lack of confidence stands in contrast to the vigour of the other residents.[90] Had James gone on to become a professional novelist, then this would have been seen as a major work of Caribbean fiction. The skill to write is evident on every page.

Next, in 1937, James brought out *World Revolution, 1917–1936, The Rise and Fall of the Communist International.* This was in many respects the most 'orthodox' of all James' Trotskyist books. Its message was that Stalin had betrayed the Russian Revolution.* The global Communist movement, James argued, was now a mere adjunct of Soviet foreign policy. It followed that an alternative movement should be built in its place. The criticisms of Stalin may be familiar now, but few agreed with James at the time. If one had to criticise his book now, it would be to say that James actually underestimated the scale of Stalin's Terror. Trotsky alone of Stalin's rivals was allowed to escape into exile, the rest of the old Bolsheviks were killed in Russia, and Trotsky himself would be murdered within three years. The scale of the killings also went far deeper into Soviet society than James or anyone in England knew. Yet ironically, James' comrades at the time tended to criticise his book in the opposite

---

* 'The economic upheaval, the social crises, had been overcome, could only have been overcome by increasing terror and the grip of the ruling caste. Nothing could stop that process now. The fate of Trotsky, Zinoviev, Kamenev, Radek, Bukharin, Rykov, Tomsky, warned all who dared to oppose. Their personal supporters would be ruthlessly cut away, they themselves would be accused of counter-revolution in the Stalinist-controlled Press, Stalin's majority would condemn them, and they would have to take the road to exile or make humiliating confessions of penitence.' C L R James, *World Revolution 1917–1936: The Rise and Fall of the Communist International* (Secker and Warburg, London: 1937) p 363.

fashion. Some felt *World Revolution* was too harsh in its treatment of the German Communists, whose failure to work in alliance with other forces James saw (rightly) as central to Hitler's seizure of power. Provocatively, that chapter is titled 'Stalin Kills the German Revolution', and hostile reviewers misrepresented James as claiming that Stalin had anticipated and planned Hitler's victory. Trotsky called *World Revolution* 'a very good book', but held that James had gone too far in treating the defeat of the Russian Revolution as 'complete'.[91] This difference of opinion with regard to the Soviet Union would be a theme of James' relationship with the Trotskyists for the next three years and beyond.

Between 1933 and 1935, James was writing for *The Guardian*. A typical piece covered the match between the South African touring party of 1935 and Lancashire. By 3.55 p.m. bad light had stopped play: 'By the time the players reached the pavilion the rain was coming down in a drizzle. A cornet-player who must have been waiting his chance began to play, "If I had a million dollars", beguiling meditation for the few hundred spectators who were being so scurvily rewarded for their enthusiasm. But though a million dollars could have done many things, there was one thing it could not possibly do, and that was stop the rain. By five minutes past four it was raining a million gallons. Even the cornet-player's game was interrupted. He began to play "God save the King". A gloomy day for everybody. At five o'clock cam the now familiar announcement: "Abandoned for the day".'[92]

James worked in the Parisian archives, studying documents from the Haitian slave revolution of the 1790s.[93] For much of that year, he was living with a fellow activist, Louise Cripps, the editor of *Nursery World* magazine. 'A born talker', is how Cripps describes James, 'this was his talent'. Before an audience 'he tended to talk in friendly person-to-person terms until those moments when his voice rose in passion and he made his most cogent points'. For a real audience, Cripps suggests, James needed more than the Trotskyists. The larger ILP provided his crowd. It was also through the Independent Labour Party, she suggests, that James met the contacts that published his books in this period. Of James' party and their views, she writes, 'We felt our work could contribute to the time when we would see Socialism spreading, when the poor would not be starving, when the homeless were given shelter, when the unemployed would be guaranteed jobs. Most of all we believed we could help working people of all nations realise that they had no interest in fighting in imperialist wars, that in each nation they would be ready to join with the underclass of other nations. Workers of the world unite: it is the only way to peace.'[94]

Cripps followed James to Paris where they met French Trotskyists. She describes helping him with the research for his later book, *The Black Jacobins*. She conveys the pleasure of his company. He was humorous. He was a kind and attentive lover. They discussed having children. But she was married; his wages could not feed three. An abortion was required. Their relationship ended, it began again. There was a second abortion. There were also political differences. James began to criticise Trotsky. Cripps did not agree with him. 'He felt that this was the result of what had happened between us. He felt that because we couldn't get married, I was taking these attitudes that did not fit into his own growing anti-Trotskyism. I knew it was not so and that it was just his masculine vanity asserting itself. He was a very proud, and in some ways, a very arrogant man. You had to agree with him on what he thought.' Cripps ended the relationship.[95]

In summer 1937 and summer 1938, James was employed at the *Glasgow Herald*. A piece for the *Herald* expressed James' disappointment with cricket at the time. Eight-ball overs had been tried. In Australia, experiments had also been conducted with the size of the wicket. Such manoeuvres, he complained, merely worked away at the edges. A better programme of reform, he suggested, would grant proper breaks to county players between matches. But even this, he admitted, would make little difference. 'Exciting cricket,' he wrote, 'depends upon exciting personalities.' The process was to some extent random: for years, cricket might indeed fail to provide stars celebrated enough to bring the crowds: 'How many competent novelists there are today! But Dickenses do not abound. There are many more good cricketers than there were, all-rounders in particular. But the men whose names fill the ground are fewer.'[96]

In 1938, James published *The Black Jacobins*: the book based on his research in the Paris archives. The history takes forward the ideas that had been used in his 1936 play. It can also be seen as the logical development of his biography of Cipriani. In *The Black Jacobins*, James took the same theme of independence, and expressed it in the field of history. His subject was the revolt of the slaves in today's Haiti. The book opens with a characteristic passage: 'Christopher Columbus landed first in the New World at the island of San Salvador, and after praising God enquired urgently for gold. The natives, Red Indians, were peaceable and friendly and directed him to Haiti, a large island (nearly as large as Ireland), rich, they said, in the yellow metal. He sailed to Haiti. One of his ships being wrecked, the Haitian Indians helped him so willingly that very little was lost and of the articles which they brought on shore not one was stolen. The Spaniards, the most advanced Europeans of their day, annexed the island, called it Hispaniola, and took the backward natives under their protection. They introduced Christianity, forced labour in mines, murder, rape, bloodhounds, strange disease, and artificial famine (by the destruction of cultivation to starve the rebellious). Those and other requirements of the higher civilisation reduced the native population from an estimated half-million, perhaps a million, to 60,000 in 15 years.'[97] The writing is sparse, James' metaphors are precise, the rhythm is that of his classical training.

By 1789, the island had been divided into two colonies. The eastern half Santo Domingo was ruled by Spain. The total population was 125,000, around one-eighth slaves. The western region, St Domingue, belonged to France. Of a total population of around 500,000, four-fifths were black African slaves, the remainder being chiefly white owners and mulattoes. In 1789, St Domingue was perhaps the richest island on earth. It exported sugar, cotton and coffee in vast quantities. This production was dependent, however, on servile conditions. Slaves worked 18-hour days. A generous owner would expect to lose one in nine workers each year, killed by over-work. *The Black Jacobins* is a history of the slave revolt that followed.

The protests began in 1791. France was then in the midst of its own revolution. The intellectuals whose writing provided the inspiration for the revolt held that all men were created equal, but they did little to demand the improvement of conditions in the French colonies. How then could the new society permit the continuation of slavery? In St Domingue, the slaves 'had heard of the revolution and had constructed it in their own images; the white slaves in France had arisen, and killed their masters, and were now enjoying the fruits of the earth.'[98] Between the needs of empire and liberty, a compromise was reached. French citizenship was extended to any mulatto in St Domingue who could prove that their father and mother had both been born in France. Some 400 were freed, while 40,000 mulattoes were left unfree, as were half a million black slaves. An insurrection broke out in the north of the island. A literate coachman, Toussaint L'Ouverture, joined the slave army. 'If the Republic, liberty and equality gave the army its morale, its centre was Toussaint himself ... His presence had that electrifying effect characteristic of great men in action.'[99] The slave army won a series of victories, and the powers responded with offers of negotiation. Toussaint's message for two years was simple: trust no owner, nor any white envoy. In 1793, however, he agreed to become an ally of France, and a French general.

In 1794, three delegates from San Domingo were sent to address the revolutionary French Assembly. The Assembly heard them enthusiastically and voted to end slavery. Yet the slave's brief triumph only encouraged the British to invade in turn. The British lost 80,000 soldiers in St Domingue, more than in all the Peninsular Wars against Napoleon. The defeat was so overwhelming that it goes unmentioned in almost all British histories of the period. Napoleon's France saw the British defeat in Machiavellian terms, welcoming the eclipse of a rival but fearing Toussaint's growing power. Bonaparte determined to replace Toussaint, first bribing his generals to rise against him, and then sending an army to complete the task.

The revolutionary regime in Haiti was weakened. An authoritarian constitution was declared. A popular rival emerged to Toussaint's left: the general ordered his execution. James's writing drips with despair at the wasting of the revolution: Toussaint 'published a series of laws surpassing in severity anything he had decreed. He introduced a rigid passport system for all classes of the population. He confined the labourers more strictly to their plantations than ever ... And while he broke the morale of the black masses, he laboured to reassure the whites.[100] Bonaparte sent his brother-in-law Leclerc to arrest Toussaint. Leclerc landed in January 1802, and Toussaint was captured in August.

Toussaint died in captivity in April 1803. Despite Toussaint's death, the slaves triumphed. Under Dessalines, the French were finally driven out, and an independent black state formed. Elsewhere, James described their victory as 'the most outstanding event in the history of the West Indies'.[101] It produced a generation of celebrated leaders. The successful establishment of a free state led inexorably to the abolition of the slave trade. It proved the possibility of self-emancipation.

Part of *The Black Jacobins'* force lies in its argument that the slave trade was not abolished as a result of the actions of a few Members of Parliament, individuals such as Wilberforce or Pitt,[102] but as a result of a racial and class struggle on the part of the slaves. Part of its great strength lies also in the method of the book. James describes Haitian society in totality, seeing the lives of the different classes from the perspective of the most oppressed. He relates developments there to political changes in conservative England and revolutionary France. The latter had of course been a great influence. 'It is impossible to understand the San Domingo revolution unless it is studied in close relationship with the revolution in France.'[103] Twenty years before such historians as Rodney Hilton, Christopher Hill, Eric Hobsbawm and E P Thompson understood the need to write 'history from below', James anticipated and matched the very best of their work.

The book has had a very wide audience since, above all in those countries where similar struggles have remained alive. The censors of apartheid South Africa would later ban *The Black Jacobins*. Yet, Scott McLemee records, it was circulated. 'Copies were scarce and the potential audience was large, so people had to improvise. One circle of activists typed up key passages and distributed them in carbon copies. Another group tore James' thick book into clusters of a few pages, to be circulated a little at a time. Members would study each fragment closely and then pass it on to the next eager reader.'[104]

If any criticism can be made of the book it is only that James's narrative (perhaps like Trotsky in his celebrated *History*) ends abruptly: with slavery defeated and an independent Haitian state. Such is our own contemporary knowledge of the post-colonial regimes that a present-day reader is left wishing that James, if not here, at least somewhere, had set out to explain the next period, when the revolutionary enthusiasm was lost; and what might have been done, so that hope might have been regained.[105]

For his next project, in 1938 James worked on translation of Boris Souvarine's biography, *Stalin*, a critical life of the dictator written by a former Trotskyist. James also published a pamphlet, A *History of Negro Revolt*. This book's theme is the history of successive black revolts, a story developed through accounts of the struggle in San Domingo, the fight for freedom from slavery in the American Civil War, uprisings in the Belgian Congo, French Congo and South Africa, the Marcus Garvey movement: 'The African bruises and breaks himself against his bars,' the pamphlet concludes, 'in the interests of freedoms wider than his own.'[106] The same year, James P Cannon,* one of the founders of American

---

* James Patrick Cannon (1890–1974) was a veteran of the Industrial Workers of the World and the Socialist Party. Chair of the American Communist Party in 1928, on a visit to the Soviet Union he read Trotsky's criticisms of the Communist International, which Moscow had circulated to foreign communists by mistake, and was persuaded by them. He founded the faction that became the Socialist Workers

Trotskyism, invited James to visit the US to speak for black liberation. 'As he travelled through the country', another biographer records, 'audiences, black and white crowded to hear him. James could speak for hours without notes, quoting facts and documents from memory. Listeners sat, enraptured by his knowledge and skills.'[107]

In April 1939, James travelled south and spent around a week with Trotsky in Mexico. Trotsky was then living in the house of the painter Diego Rivera, although following the discovery of Trotsky's affair with Rivera's lover Frida Kahlo, Trotsky had been asked to leave and soon would. 'I have not met Diego,' James wrote, 'There is a split between him and L.T.; L.T. is moving out of his house. There have been letters in the press and a general mess. D. R. has left the IV [the Fourth International: the alliance of Trotskyist parties round the world].'[108] For the moment, however, this was a romantic setting, charged with political intrigue. In Rivera's house, James and Trotsky discussed the slogans that should be used to lead the black movement in the United States. The background to their discussions lay in the previous tactics for black liberation adopted by other Marxists. The American Communists advanced the idea that blacks were a separate nation, so it followed that they should be allowed to form an independent black state. The strength of this position was that it acknowledged the racism within the United States. Certainly in the 1930s, the Communists were able to play a leading role in a number of black struggles. But the Communist position also had weaknesses. One lay with the slogan of independence: was it viable? Another problem was more general. Through this period, the Communists tended to vacillate, adopting left and then right positions to suit the demands of the International. We have already seen the damage that similar shifts had caused to the Communists' relationship with activists such as Padmore. One year's successful anti-racist work could then be undermined by another years'

Party, which with 1000 members was by 1939 the largest Trotskyist party in the world. Cannon remained a major figure in international Trotskyist circles into the mid-1960s.

more cautious line. In response, the American Trotskyists attempted to argue for a more consistent anti-racist politics. But Trotsky feared that his comrades were too passive in this fight.

Both James and Trotsky were thinking towards a new conception of liberation. Traditionally, Marxists had tended to think of oppressed peoples as a nation, whose equality required the foundation of a new state. But 'although the Negro is nationalist to his heart and is perfectly right to be so,'[109] the black population of North America was a race, not a nation. What black people sought was not an independent society within America, but something conceptually simpler, an equal, non-racist United States.*

In his meeting with Trotsky, James spoke of the need for independent black organisation. His idea was that black struggle was spontaneously militant. The right approach was to found organisations to encourage and develop further protests. In the process, the Trotskyists would quickly learn all the politics they required. Hearing his comrade speak, Trotsky appears to have been struck by a certain contrast between James' tactical ability and the weakness of his strategy. The clear identification with black struggle placed James to the head of his contemporaries, but what was the goal? Here is James' formula: 'The Negro must be won for socialism. There is no other way out for him in America or elsewhere. But he must be won on the basis of his own experience and activity.

---

* 'In Africa and in the West Indies we advocate self-determination because a large majority of the people want it. In Africa the great mass of the people look upon self-determination as a restoration of their independence ... In America, the situation is different. The Negro desperately wants to be an American citizen. He says, "I have been here from the beginning. I did all the work here in the early days. Jews, Poles, Italians, Swedes and others come here and have all the privileges. You say that some of the Germans are spies. I will never spy. I have nobody for whom to spy. And yet you exclude me from the army and from the privileges of citizenship."' C L R James in conversation with Leon Trotsky. Cited in G Breitman (ed.), *Leon Trotsky on Black Nationalism and Self-Determination* (Pathfinder Press, New York: 1967), p 24.

There is no other way for him to learn, nor for that matter, for any other group of toilers! If he wanted self-determination, then however reactionary it might be in any other respect, it would be the business of the revolutionary party to raise that slogan ... But the Negro, fortunately for socialism, does not want self-determination.'[110]

Leon Trotsky identified a number of confusions in his comrade. First, he was unsure whether C L R James wanted to see the removal of the slogan of self-determination from both the short- and long-term programme of the left. Secondly, Trotsky rejected James' passing use of the term 'reactionary' to describe those black struggles that had the goal of separation. It seemed too close to him to that 'socialism' which identified black nationalism and white racism as deserving equal criticism, and therefore sided in practice with the privileged against the oppressed. Where he agreed was in James' advocacy of a number of practical steps to transform the Trotskyists' work among black Americans. James argued that his comrades should organise anti-racist study groups, a campaign in industry among black workers, housing and rent campaigns, a campaign to expose the racism of the Republican and Democratic Parties, a speaking circuit with black radicals from South or West Africa to tour the United States, and an electoral campaign.[111]

It is difficult to do justice to this meeting. Although James later claimed to have disagreed with and surpassed Trotsky, the outcome was more complex. James rejected some and accepted other parts of Trotsky's analysis. Above all, he learned from the great personal authority of the man: 'Although we disagreed, I was tremendously impressed. Trotsky started with the analysis, international, political and philosophical. But the action, the activity, always followed. I got a glimpse of what Bolshevism of the old school meant.'[112] Another subsequent essay, on 'Trotsky's Place in History', reflected the older man's influence on James: 'Being determines consciousness. In the struggle for socialism he strides through the world, a titan among men, excelling in every field he touched. An exile half his life, persecuted as no man has been persecuted, he lived the fullest life of any human being hitherto. The field of being, which he chose, developed his consciousness to a pitch reached by few men. That consciousness he did his best to pass on to us.'[113]

On leaving Trotsky, C L R James used the opportunity to visit the southern states of America. The racism he observed was more brutal than anything he had seen before, either in the Caribbean or with Learie Constantine in Britain. In other ways, America challenged his understanding of the world. Britain was a declining economic power, while America was on the rise. At the time of his conversion to Trotskyism, James had adopted the view that there was no point seeking transformation in Trinidad alone, any protest there would inevitably be crushed by London. But the same approach could be extended. What could a victorious labour movement achieve in Britain, if even after a revolution in London, America was still run along capitalist lines?

A growing sense of the narrowness of English society was accompanied by a frustration even with the game of cricket. Frank Woolley retired at the end of the 1938 season. James was elegiac: 'He gave to thousands and thousands of his countrymen a conception of the beautiful which artists struggle to capture in paint and on canvas.'[114] But the problem was no longer merely an absence of exciting personalities. The emphasis was no longer on brilliance or inspiration, but on sheer hard work. Bradman had become the game's dominant personality, and the batsman was no artist. For James, Bradman's gifts lay in 'nervous stamina and concentration': they were virtues, but not the ones that appealed. The contest between England and Australia continued, 'if Bradman continued his portentous career, a way of life, a system of morals, faced the possibility of disgrace and defeat just at the particular time when more than ever it needed the stimulus of victory and prestige ... The spirit of Bodyline was not exorcised',[115] and faced with the choice between England and Australia, James could take neither side.

In later interviews, James claimed that he had intended to return to England in time for the 1939 cricket season and that the first signs of the impending war were enough to make travel impossible. But in spring 1939, there were still ships travelling between the two continents.

Elsewhere James would claim that a new friend, Raya Dunayevskaya, had been crucial to his decision to stay. 'She had come to the conclusion that I was the man to remain in the United States [to be the] head of the Trotskyist movement as a whole. I was in doubt whether to go or to stay. Raya was insistent that I stay.'[116] Whether or not this memory is right, the decision was made. Just as James had previously outgrown Trinidad, he had become weary of Britain. It was in America that he now intended to make his name.

5

The Struggle for Happiness

(Previous page) Leon Trotsky *(third from right)* and Frida Kahlo *(third from left)* arriving in Tampico, Mexico in 1937.

James remained in the United States for 15 years (1938–53), roughly twice as long as his first period of willing exile in England. In America, James found himself right at the heart of historic events. He believed passionately in world revolution. Nowhere would be more central to the prospects of that revolt than America. Here, capitalism was at the very height of its development. Here were the potential forces of rebellion, the multi-racial working class of the Northern cities, and the oppressed black masses of the American South. In America, we have the evidence of James' friendships, documented in surviving letters, and especially in correspondence with his future wife Constance Webb. James also attempted to grasp the outlines of his new home through his membership of the Socialist Workers Party, then the main Trotskyist group in the country.

Even for his most sympathetic biographers, James's long immersion in the small-group politics of the Marxist left is a matter of surprise (or regret). James had so many urgent things to say; why then did he waste so much time on what his biographers often treat as the sad conspiracies of a fringe? One answer is that James felt genuinely invigorated by the politics he encountered. Small as it was, the Trotskyist movement was connected to other left-wing milieus. It gave James opportunities to speak. It gave him the chance to meet people new to the movement, filled with the joys at the first realisation of the possibilities of profound change. It introduced James to other people whose experiences were simply different from his: because they worked for a living, because they had studied for academic qualifications, because they were the product of different migrant experiences. His comrades helped to shape James. He learned from them. He shared their conviction that a period of war must be followed by an age of revolution. The activist milieu provided James with the intense friendships of others who had lived through the same experiences: the elation at the well-packed meeting, the fear of state repression, of blacklisting, detention or deportation. Those who struggle together learn to trust each other: it is a deep comradeship rarely experienced anywhere else in life.

'Most of his friends and admirers today', writes Grace Lee Boggs, an ally from this period and later, 'find it difficult to understand how C. L. R., who had already made a name for himself as the author of *The Black Jacobins* and as a cricket correspondent when he came to the United States in 1938, was content to spend the next fifteen years living and working in obscurity inside the small Trotskyite parties, writing and speaking under pseudonyms like J. R. Johnson and AAB. My own view is that they were the happiest and most productive years of his long and extraordinarily productive life.'[117]

As well as Boggs, we have encountered Raya Dunayevskaya, who James said had persuaded him to remain in America. But the most important relationship from this period was his romance with Constance Webb. Radicalised by many experiences, including a hatred of her own father's racism, Webb joined the Trotskyists in 1935, at the age of just 15. She heard James speak for the first time in Los Angeles, three years later. Years afterwards, she could still recall, 'He was over six feet two inches, slim, but not thin, with long legs. He walked easily, with his shoulders level. His head appeared to be on a stalk, held high with the chin titled forward and up, which made it seem that his body was led by a long neck, curved forward like that of a racehorse in the slip. Shoulders, chest, and legs were powerful and he moved decisively. But, as with highly trained athletes, the tension was concentrated and tuned, so that he gave the impression of enormous ease. He was without self-consciousness, simply himself, which showed in the way he moved, and one recognised a special quality.'[118]

James and Webb met, with Webb telling James of her frustrations with the Trotskyists in Fresno. 'There did not seem to be any particular interest in the condition and treatment of blacks. And there were only one or two black men; they might come to our socials but not to meetings, and they did not join.' James spoke about his pending meeting with Trotsky, and his desire to secure the older man's backing for a campaign within the SWP against racism. Webb kept silent certain doubts. In a striking phrase, she later wrote, 'James was very inexperienced when it came to understanding the complexity of race relations, not only between black and white, but among Jews, Mexicans, Asians, Italians.' He invited her to set up a reading group among her friends, and in another typical touch, to write a pamphlet. Their conversation was always one of equals. How easy it would be to forget that James was more than twice Webb's age.[119]

James fell in love with Webb. It was an unlikely alliance. She was young, married and white. She was living in Fresno, while James was intending to see Mexico, the South and leave. Each of these barriers was high. A mixed-race union in particular could barely have been forgiven in the America of the time. Between 1938 and 1944, James and Webb corresponded. Throughout this same period, Webb was active on the left, divorced two husbands and modelled for Salvador Dali, whom she stopped working for after the artist humiliated her sexually. Had he known her politics, or she his, it is likely that their creative collaboration would have been even briefer than it was.

In April 1939, James confessed to Webb that he had only just begun his study of Marx's economic manuscripts. 'And now for *Das Kapital.* My dear young woman I have some news for you. One reputed Marxist, having thought over his past life, and future prospects, decided that what he needed was a severe and laborious study of, guess! *The Bible*? Wrong? *Ferdinand the Bull*? Wrong again. Not *das Kapital*? Right. (Loud and prolonged cheering, all rise and sing the 'Internationale'.) I bought the book a few days ago in pesos and have got down to it. (This is only volume one by the way. There are two more. You made a mistake when you thought you had read them all.) I shall read those three volumes and nothing will stop me but a revolution.'[120]

Shortly after, James travelled to Mexico to meet Trotsky. He told Webb that Trotsky had supported his line on race. Trotsky was 'the keenest of the keen on the N[egro] question ... The Negroes as the most oppressed must become the very vanguard of the revolution.' Leaving Mexico behind, James wrote but did not send a long 'love letter'. He sent Webb a short story instead based on his feelings of limbo, waiting for his ship to arrive in New Orleans. Webb confided to James that her marriage was over. James became more expansive. On returning to New York, however, his letters became more guarded. James expressed only his deep frustrations at the many pointless squabbles that divided his party's leadership. 'I am not going into the rights and the wrongs of the case but under such circumstances it is pathetic to see each side laying the blame on the other.' Then in December 1939, James' visa expired, and he was forced to go underground. Political campaigns focused on the war in Europe now took up all James' time. Gone was the earlier optimism. Following Trotsky's death in August 1940, he wrote, 'It is adversity that tests and makes people. It is easy to sail along when everything is flowing with you. But now we need courage.'[121]

All the time, C L R James' public life was dominated by his political activity. When he joined the SWP in 1938, it was the largest Trotskyist organisation in the world. Bohemian and outward looking, the party recruited a number of prominent intellectuals, not least in New York. Yet almost immediately, the SWP was rent by a deep split. It concerned the question of how to understand the Stalinist states. As James would later write, of his party's leaders, 'Their chief concern, as was typical among politicians in the thirties, was to get to the policy right. Their idea was that if you had the correct policies that you were able to play the correct party, and by means of the correct party ultimately that you would lead the revolution to success.'[122] This was an important criticism, and one that James himself would not always live by later. Cannon and his critics alike were characterised by the tendency to exaggerate ideas at the expense of activity, to think that all that was needed was the right analysis or programme, when the problem for the left is rarely one of formulating the perfect programme, but of convincing people rather that you or your allies have a sense of how to make the right changes happen. The task is always one of making abstract theory real.

Until 1939, the American Trotskyists had assumed that any world war must be a struggle primarily between Germany and Russia. Yet the 1939 Stalin-Hitler pact seemed to throw this formula into doubt. Trotsky himself continued to insist that the Soviet Union was worthy of defence, while his supporters also argued that Russia remained some sort of 'workers' state'. Max Shachtman, James Burnham and other rebels replied that Russia was a hostile, 'bureaucratic collectivist' or 'totalitarian' entity. James followed Shachtman,* joining his Workers Party in 1940. Webb was now in Los Angeles, and also signed up with the Workers Party. Indeed she lists some of the allies that were moving towards their positions at the this time, including the writers Hal Draper, Irving Howe, Dwight MacDonald, James T Farrell and Saul Bellow.† This was a remarkable, talented generation of writers, many of them based in New York. Like recruits like: such figures reflected the literary instincts

---

* At the age of 19, Max Shachtman (1904–72) was a leader of the youth section of the Communist Party, and an alternate member of the CP's central committee. Five years later, he was with James P Cannon one of the founders of American Trotskyism. In 1940, he broke from Cannon, arguing that the Soviet Union was a bureaucratic collectivist society, one that socialists should in no way support. During the post-war period, Shachtman was increasingly reconciled to the politics of American liberalism, supporting the war effort in Vietnam, and calling for socialists to join the Democrats. Such former Shachtmanites as Irving Kristol, Nathan Glazer, and Sidney Hook, were by the mid-1960s prominent American neo-conservatives.

† Hal Draper (1914–90) was a writer and activist and a leading figure in the Berkeley Free Speech campaign of the 1960s. After breaking with Shachtman he helped to found an Independent Socialist Club, which became a party, the Independent Socialists (later the International Socialists). His best known works include a pamphlet *The Two Souls of Socialism* (1960) and a multi-volume study of *Karl Marx's Theory of Revolution*. He was also a founder of the journal, *New Politics*.

Dwight MacDonald (1906–82) was a journalist for *Time* and *Fortune* magazines, a supporter of Shachtman, a writer for the New York journal *Partisan Review,* later an anarchist and then a supporter of America in its Cold War struggles with Russia. Later still he was a fierce opponent of the Vietnam War.

Saul Bellow (1915–2005) was one of the great American novelists of the 20th century, a youthful Trotskyist, and subsequently an often-conservative commentator on the American 'culture wars'. His books include *Dangling Man* (1944), *The Victim* (1947), *The Adventures of Augie March* (1953), *Henderson the Rain King* (1959), *Herzog* (1964) and *Humboldt's Gift* (1975).

of the party's leader Shachtman. The Workers Party took the youth and the intellectuals. Led by James Cannon, the parent SWP retained many of the working-class members.

A moment of opportunity was followed by a period of defeats. One early defection set the tone for the future. James Burnham* left the Workers Party in 1940, defending an abstract-sounding position, that a 'managerial revolution' had taken place in Russia, in 1917, 1921 or 1928. Behind this phrase Burnham was saying that the left should support the war effort. The only choice remaining to the world was between American liberalism and German or Soviet fascism. The left had a moral duty to endorse American liberalism. But if socialists endorsed the US then would they remain revolutionary? Was there no choice other than to back either of the empires? 'A man of remarkable intellect and great strength of character,' James told Webb, 'has crawled out of the revolutionary movement by the back door; today stands nowhere; tomorrow will have to stand with the bourgeoisie, for society offers you no third choice in this crisis.' James was right. Within months of leaving the party, Burnham had become a prominent conservative.[123]

Romance flourished despite everything. After a year apart, James and Webb met up again in New York in spring 1940. Courtship was resumed at a restaurant on MacDougall Street just North of Washington Square. Connie, the owner, ran what Constance Webb termed, 'the first integrated restaurant in New York'. 'If Connie noticed someone who seemed hostile to white women dining with black men or black women dining with white men, she marched up to the table and invited the person to

---

* James Burnham (1905–87) taught philosophy at New York University. He came into contact with American Trotskyism in 1934, and became one of the best-known writers associated with the Socialist Workers Party. He left at the time of the split that produced the Workers Party. His 1941 book *The Managerial Revolution* argued that the coming war would be between liberalism and socialism; Americans must choose the former. By the 1950s, he was a senior editor at the Conservative *National Review*.

leave. She was a well-built, rather husky woman, and could be a formidable opponent.' James sometimes cooked at home. His favourite dishes were okra, salt cod and callaloo.

James' friends included the authors Richard Wright,* Ralph Ellison and Chester Himes. He was taken by Wright's novel *Native Son*, praising it in a review in the language that he had previously reserved for Trotsky's *History:* 'Black Bigger Thomas, native, stifled by and inwardly rebellious against white America's treatment of him, by accident murders a white girl ... Before he is sentenced to death, the sincere efforts of two white Communists to save him teach him that all whites are not his enemies, that he is not alone, that there is a solidarity of all the oppressed ... It was the bursting pride of a spirit long cramped and oppressed that found itself free at last. All students of revolutionary history know it, the legions of Spartacus, Cromwell's Ironsides, the Paris enrages ...'[124]

Constance Webb, too, was close to Richard Wright. 'Both of us were passionately interested in the nuances of racial prejudice. We spent hours examining its various forms and the incidents we experienced or observed. During such discussions Nello [C L R James] sat quietly by, listening intently. Later he said he was astonished both at our preoccupation with the subject and our closeness, after all, he said, "You are white, Dick is black, and I am black. But I am out of it entirely when the two of you get together." He went on to explain that in Trinidad he had never been particularly aware of being black and as a result the subject had not interested him. In London, Amy Ashwood Garvey, the first wife of Marcus Garvey, told him, "You are not a Negro". She, of course, had the experience of the US as a reference.'[125] It was the same feeling that

---

* Richard Wright (1908–60) grew up in Jackson, Mississippi, moving to Chicago, where he joined the Communist Party. He was for a time the Harlem editor of the Communists' paper the *Daily Worker*. His most famous book, *Native Son* was published in 1940. Wright left the Communist Party in 1942. His later books include *Black Boy* (1945), *The Outsider* (1953) and a collection of stories, *Eight Men* (1960).

Webb had recorded after her first meeting with James: that even after several years spent living in the country he saw the American social codes from the outside and was still separated from the people whose cause he championed.

James' work on black liberation brought him into contact with another dissident, Rae Spiegel, also known as Raya Dunayevskaya,* who we have already encountered. Dunayevskaya was a Jewish woman, born in the Ukraine and brought to the United States as a child. She joined the revolutionary movement young and in the 1920s was involved with the American Negro Labor Congress and the newspaper *Negro Champion*. Dunayevskaya had also worked as Trotsky's secretary in Mexico. She was conscious of her own standing as an important figure in the Trotskyist movement, and resented the sexism of her party, which closed opportunities off to woman such as her; she also had difficulty keeping friends among the other woman comrades, few of whom were as confident in their criticisms of the men. 'A major grievance', recalls Webb, 'was that the leadership, all male, treated women as their handmaidens, leaving them to do all the mimeographing, the serving and cleaning up after making coffee, and sometimes the sweeping of the offices. Raya had rebelled and was not very well liked by many of the women.' Dunayevskaya was married, Webb continues, 'so for many years I did not realize that she and Nello had sometimes been joined in more ways than politics.'[126]

As a consequence of having chosen to over-stay illegally in America, James did not dare speak publicly and could write only under a

---

* Raya Dunayevskaya (1910–87) followed James P Cannon when he left the Communist Party in 1928 to found America's first Trotskyist group. Collaborating with James after the split between the Socialist Workers Party and the Workers Party, Dunayevskaya continued to ally with James until their own split in 1955. Her best-known books include *Marxism and Freedom* (1958), *Philosophy and Revolution* (1973), and *Rosa Luxemburg, Women's Liberation, and Marx's Philosophy of Revolution* (1982).

pseudonym. In the socialist press, he signed himself 'J. R. Johnson', and Dunayevskaya published as 'Freddie Forrest', hence their friendship led to the formation of a faction that was soon known as the 'Johnson-Forest Tendency'. Constance Webb, living freely in New York, and surrounded now by a circle of actors, among whom a looser socialist politics was common, was not impressed. 'When Nello told me the name,' Webb recalls, 'I couldn't help laughing and blurted out. "Tendency! What does that mean, for goodness sake?"'[127]

While James was best known on the left for his views on race, Dunayevskaya was first of all a critic of Trotskyist attitudes towards the Soviet Union. Since the early 1940s, both she and James had maintained that Russia was state capitalist.[128] At stake in the arguments were key questions for the left: should socialists support Russia or America? Even if they were hostile to it, was there anything that socialists could learn from the Russian experience? To understand the importance of this theory we should recall that Lenin and his allies had taken power just two decades previously. The USSR presented itself to the world as a successful Communist society, one in which class differences no longer existed, or were on the verge of dying out. When workers in the West thought of Marxism, their first response was to think of Russia. Yet under Stalin, Russia had become a new tyranny: the labour camps held hundreds of thousands of inmates. Whole populations were starved to death. Old Communists were arrested and killed. The suffering of the Russian workers was extreme.

The state capitalist analysis was a partial rejection of the approach developed by Trotsky, who had insisted through all his life that Russian remained in some residual fashion 'socialist'. Even if deformed, the state belonged to the workers. The key text in which he had developed this approach was his book, *The Revolution Betrayed*. Here Trotsky had considered the possibility that Russia might one day become state capitalist, but refused to accept the process was already complete. If large parts of the economy were controlled by the state, he insisted, the result could not be capitalism, but must still be in some distorted fashion socialist.

The bureaucracy defended the victories of October, he claimed. It did not seek the restoration of private property.[129]

One point at which James seemed to have the better of the argument was when he insisted that the Russian working class operated no practical control over 'their' state. The essence of Trotsky's argument seemed to be that state ownership was incompatible with production for profit. Yet what else had Stalin accomplished than a system run for accumulation's sake, in which the bureaucracy thrived, and all other classes suffered? 'The [Russian] working class has been reduced to a state of pauperisation,' James wrote, 'slavery, and degradation unequalled in modern Europe. The real wages of the workers are approximately one-half of what they were in 1913. A bureaucracy holds all economic and political power. To continue to call the Russian workers the ruling class is to make a statement without meaning.'[130] The state capitalist theory may have been a partial break from the letter of Trotsky's argument, but in other senses it could be said to have affirmed or even completed Trotskyism.[131] In arguing that the sole question in judging how to evaluate Russia was not planning, but a simpler issue, who ruled?, James was restoring democracy as the key idea of socialism.

We can see the significance of the argument if we think from the perspective of those who supported the Soviet Union. They called themselves socialists, in Britain or America, and they argued for power to be taken by the people. Yet in Russia they supported a system of dictatorial, personal rule. Marxism was supposed to be a science of working-class struggle. In Russia, the working class had no greater enemy than the Soviet state. Communists in Britain and America found themselves arguing for democracy in one country, but for tyranny in another country. Politically and morally they were debased. Even the Trotskyists, James argued, fell into something like the same trap: they shared the vestiges of loyalty to the USSR. Backing for dictatorship diminished them too.

Breaking from the other Trotskyists on the question of Russia, C L R James and Raya Dunayevskaya came to question other orthodoxies as well. The work of the group included the first English-language translation of Marx's philosophical manuscripts from the 1840s. James' thoughts on Marxism and its origin in philosophy were collected in a 1948 manuscript, *Notes on Dialectics*. A number of people were involved in the discussions that shaped the text, including James, Dunayevskaya, a recently graduated student Grace Lee, who had a doctorate in philosophy, and a worker called Johnny Zupern, who had a talent for comprehending abstractions. Dunayevskaya could read the Russian texts, Lee the German, and James the French. The brilliance of *Notes on Dialectics* was that it drew attention towards Marx's dialectic,* the method that Karl Marx had learned from Hegel's *Science of Logic* and upon which the socialist philosopher had built his entire theory of change.[132]

Especially given its difficult, technical subject, *Notes on Dialectics* is beautifully written and often feels like the work of a contemporary. There are deliberate repetitions, humorous asides. The words are the spoken language of a friend. Reading the book, you can tell that C L R James knows that Hegel is the hardest part of Karl Marx's inheritance, and therefore the most necessary to explain. The book delights in Hegel's method, bringing out the energy of dialectics, the sense that Marxism is above all a creative study in change. 'That is the aim of [Hegel's] Logic, for the thousandth time, how to keep out of the fixed, limited, finite categories. Hegel is doing just this, in a constantly more concrete manner, page after page. That is all. But what an all! To get out of the clutching hands of fixed categories. It isn't easy. Precisely because we have to get them fixed and precise before we can do anything.'[133]

---

* The dialectic: a philosophical method designed to find truth through the negation of error. In one form, the Socratic dialectic, a thesis leads to a contradiction, and an alternative point of view, an antithesis emerges. This too is shown to be false, and only then a third, correct, statement appears: the synthesis. The Socratic method was taken over by the German philosopher Hegel, who used it to structure his argument that the history of the world was the unfolding story of man's growing self-consciousness. Marx in turn employed the method, arguing (for example) that out of the conflict between capitalists and workers, a new socialist society would appear.

Two particular moments are essential to understanding the book. One is Trotsky's death in 1940, and the legacy he left to the movement, which *Notes on Dialectics* identifies as being the false understanding of Stalinist Russia. Trotsky's mistake, James argues, was to write as if the society of the immediate post-revolutionary period had still been preserved (if only in part) in the state forms of high Stalinism. His was 'a purely abstract argument', James claimed, 'finite, fixed, limited. Stalin, empirical, doing whatever came naturally altered his categories ruthlessly, whatever Leninist names he called them ... Trotsky lost himself in greater and greater abstractions, until ultimately he did not expose, he *justified* the bureaucracy.'[134]

The second moment concerns Trotsky's 1917 ally, Lenin. The older man's isolation at the time of the 1914–18 war had caused him to re-read Hegel and in that moment, James argues, the Russian Marxist realised the incompleteness of all other socialisms since Marx's death. A dialectical method gave Lenin the confidence to argue for Russia's revolutionary defeat in the war. It was the necessary theoretical prelude to the victory of the October Revolution. 'In reading [Hegel's] *On Quality in the Doctrine of Being*, Lenin writes in very large writing. LEAP. LEAP. LEAP. LEAP. LEAP. This obviously hit him hard. He wanted it stuck down in his head, to remember it, always ... Hegel is bored to tears at people who keep looking for signs and the "the mere magnitudinal" as proof. Lenin did not fasten on this for nothing. He said, "Turn the Imperialist War into Civil War." How many sincere opponents of imperialism recoiled in horror. "Too rash, too crude, not now." (Trotsky was among them). Lenin would not budge. The socialist movement against imperialism would establish itself on the concrete transition – the opposition to the monstrous evil of the war. He didn't have to wait to see anything. That was there. It would LEAP up.'[135] The moral of this story may have seemed clear to James and his allies. As a dialectical method enabled Lenin to escape his isolation in 1914, so it might do the same for them. The difference, of course, is that Lenin's wartime isolation was only passing. The acknowledged leader of a party whose membership had stood in recent times at more then 50,000 people, Lenin's name was known to the mass of the Russian workers. This obstacle was not popular indifference to Bolshevism but state repression. For all its undoubted quality, then, there is a false tone in *Notes on Dialectics*. Thought is treated as the 'link between human beings and things'. The world can be understood only by creating universal categories: 'You must know categorisation in general, movement in general, changes in categories in general, and then you can examine the object ... and work out its categories, its form of movement, its method of change etc., always conscious of the general laws as exemplified in the particular concrete.'[136] James and Dunayevskaya seem to follow Marx's method of ascending from the abstract to the concrete. But the adherence is formal. So much time is spent in dealing with the abstract that the concrete remains unexplored.

In a typical passage, the authors repeat that Trotsky had been wrong in refusing to analyse Stalinist Russia as a state capitalist society. James and Dunayevskaya ask what fault there was in Trotsky's method, which might explain this recurring failure? Their diagnoses are several; Trotsky adopted a linear, rather than a dialectical method. Trotsky looked to the subjective, corruption, when he should have detected objective economic fact. 'As I think over Trotsky's writings, I can see this sequence of cause and effect in an endless chain. This happened, *then* the other, *then* the Stalinist bureaucracy did this; then; and so he keeps up an endless series of explanations, fascinating, brilliant, full of insights and illuminations, to crash into his catastrophic blunders at the end. Every illustration by Trotsky of the criminal blunders of the Stalinist intervention on the world proletarian struggle is in reality a deadly blow against the capacity, the historical capacity of the proletariat. We, on the other hand, who show that the Stalinist cause could create the mighty worldwide *effect* because it elicited *class* forces hostile to the proletariat and inherent in capitalist society at this stage of its development, we restore to the proletarian struggle the historical objectivity of the struggle of the classes with social roots. We finish away with the demoralizing, in fact self-destroying theory that everything would have been all right, but for the intervention of Stalinist corruption.'[137]

The authors' conclusions are politically superior to Trotsky's. In defining the Soviet Union as state capitalist, James and other thinkers facilitated the later rise of new forces on the left untainted by any need to apologise for dictatorship. This chief criticism of Trotsky in the above passage, however, concerns not his conclusions but his method. *Notes on Dialectics* accuses Trotsky of failing to grasp the economic. Read Trotsky's *Revolution Betrayed*, and you will see that the Russian writer's argument was based on a sustained study of Soviet statistics, in so far as they were available. The authors of *Notes on Dialectics*, by contrast, seem to believe that simply by proclaiming 'Look, Russia is State Capitalist', they have demonstrated an argument, when the argument remains to be proved.

One strength of the book was its humour. James 'was playful', Constance Webb writes, 'and tried out many roles, as if donning different costumes ... One time he found a cheap ring, the type given away in Crackerjack boxes, gold-coloured, glass faking a diamond, a very ornate affair. He promptly put it on his little finger, where it shone against his dark skin and appeared even cheaper. And on a man it looked even more ridiculous. When he saw I disliked it, he kept wearing it for days, admiring on its beauty whenever I was around.'[138]

As James was penning this personal credo, his relationship with Webb was reaching crisis point. Despite their several years' courtship, there was still no clear agreement between them. James suggested that they should leave town together and spend a week in each other's company. She declined. 'I loved Nello as I would my father or a younger brother.' Webb wanted the two of them to stop seeing one another. James' reply began with a self-appraisal. 'Look at me. I am 45. I am not a healthy person. My hands shake. My beard is terribly grey. I can very often look my age. I don't know when I will be yanked from here and told to get out with no possibility of ever coming back. I am a Negro, which means that an association with me will be tough for anyone.' The declaration of love was written with the same insistent dialectic as James on philosophy, with full conviction, to strip away all doubts.' If you gave me only a part of yourself, then it is my business to make you come further. I can't see it any other way. That is a matter not of our future, it is a matter of *now*. That is and must be the correct relationship between us. Dig into yourself and see what barriers and constrictions are created, how wrong it is, for you to carry in your mind, to have carried, the conception that you had to be on guard lest you deceive me. Sure I know you had cause. I know you were fighting instincts and doubts and fears, oh! Yes fears too. (Don't you think I have them too?) But at any rate they must go.'[139]

James and Webb married in May 1946. 'Nello and I did not reach that state of indifference in which we would be bored by lovemaking, possibly because he travelled so much and each homecoming was like a honeymoon.' The attentions of the FBI left them both exhausted. Webb also complained that there were other people in James' life that he refused to discuss with her. 'The eight years of letters from Nello,' she wrote at the time, 'had made me feel like a princess. Suddenly I was Cinderella; the ball was over and I was relegated to cleaning the kitchen.' James had a capacity for silence that left Webb feeling isolated and alone. The advocate of a new humanity was himself diminished, she maintained, by his sheer inability to merge his personal and political life. 'Each was important, but it often seemed that his politics stemmed the flow of his creativity. Why else was he so happy and able to turn out thousands of words seemingly without effort when he was away from his group?' A son, C L R James Jnr. or 'Nobbie' was born in April 1949. Yet the birth of a child showed only the impossibility of their relationship. Both James and Webb had affairs through the marriage, Webb once, James repeatedly, and their relationship came to an end with James' later incarceration.[140]

From the early 1940s, James also appears to have been planning his exit from the Trotskyist movement. In this process there was a certain fusing of arguments. James was critical both of Leninist parties in general, and of the American Trotskyists in particular. The SWP contained at its height barely 1,000 members, or one member for every hundred thousand American adults. Its rivals on the American left were even smaller. From such an isolated beginning, the party went on to shed disdainfully its few remaining links to the US working class. The 1940 split led to the defection of the intellectuals. The trade union cadres left afterwards, in waves. Those people who remained in the leadership were less capable of thinking beyond the past than the dissident James. By 1947, James and his allies in the Johnson-Forest Tendency had the support of some six-dozen activists, representing a sizeable bloc within American Trotskyism. A year later, the Tendency re-joined the Socialist Workers Party. Yet the comrades found no shelter there. The SWP gave critical support to Tito in his conflict with Stalin, but James would not agree with them. The supporters of the Johnson-Forest Tendency described the hostility they received, 'hysteria, red eyes and shaking fists'.[141] In 1951, James and his comrades left the SWP for the last time.

James remained a Marxist. One pamphlet from the 1950s *Every Cook Can Govern* is a passionate defence of direct democracy. James argued that unfettered direct popular control could form the basis for a new government in later times.* The public assembly of all citizens was the government. 'Perhaps the most striking thing about Greek Democracy was that the administration (and there were immense administrative problems) was organised upon the basis of what is known as sortition, or, more easily, selection by lot. The vast majority of Greek officials were chosen by a method which amounted to putting names into a hat and appointing the one whose names came out. Now the average CIO bureaucrat or Labor Member of Parliament in Britain would fall into a fit if it was suggested to him that any worker selected at random could

---

* 'Every Greek city was an independent state. At its best, in the city-state of Athens, the public assembly of all the citizens made all important decisions on such questions as peace or war. They listened to the envoys of foreign powers and decided what their attitude should be to what these foreign powers had sent to say. They dealt with all serious questions of taxation. They appointed the generals who should lead them in time and war. They organised the administration of the state, appointed officials and kept check on them.' C L R James, *Every Cook Can Govern: A Study of Democracy in Ancient Greece* (Correspondence, Detroit: 1956) p 2.

do the work he is doing. But that was precisely the guiding principle of Greek Democracy. And this form of government under which flourished the greatest civilisation the world has ever known ... The principle of Greek democracy was this, that every single member of society, the tailor, the shoemaker, the factory worker, the cook, as well as an educated nobleman or merchant, was fully able to take part in the government of the state. The Greek democrats believed this and practiced it to the extreme limit.'[142] James was arguing for the democratic principle and one still worthy of achievement many years on.

On what terms, though, was democracy defended? 'The elite party, or as it is more familiarly known, the Vanguard Party, is the most advanced form of representative government. The Communists with their theory of "the party" constituting of the most devoted ... are the most shameless theorists and practitioners of it today. The Trotskyites, imitating the Communists in this as in everything else, are the comedians of the theory of the Vanguard Party.'[143] If representative democracy was a process by which the rich offered the majority nothing more than the mere hint of real choice, then James was right to identify this deceit as a great fraud. But it was ludicrous to couple that true insight to the further suggestion that the worst culprits in this sordid game were neither the political class in Washington, nor their equivalents in Russia, but the petty Stalins of Western Communism. Again, although the barb against Trotskyism may have provided a certain psychological satisfaction, what use was it to bait them in the 1950s, when the whole world party of the Fourth International was less than 5,000 strong?

I have argued elsewhere that the most interesting of 20th-century Marxists were those that emerged within and to some extent against disciplined Marxist parties. It was precisely the tension between the individual instincts of the experienced activist or writer and the need for collective work on the part of the group, which enabled them to develop truly creative positions. Certainly, James was a freer man than the leaders of the other Trotskyist factions. Tony Bogues' biography is termed 'Caliban's freedom', linking James to Shakespeare's near-mythical figure of the slave in revolt. It is a fine metaphor, which captures something of the epic grandeur of James' socialist vision. Yet as much as James gained in his independence from a party, he also lost by the same route. Afterwards, James did again establish parties, but he was invariably the leader. The departure made him 'large, containing multitudes'.[144] It also contributed to his isolation.

In 1949 and 1953, James contemplated a full-length biographical study of Shakespeare. He saw the theme of the plays as being the contradiction between the search for individual fulfilment and the need for social life. On this reading, the theme of *Hamlet* was the struggle for individual knowledge, with Hamlet's soliloquy standing for the isolation of the intellectual. *Lear*, James went on, was Shakespeare's great play, and Poor Tom his greatest character. Poor Tom is the witness to Lear's descent into madness, a fury he explains as Lear's inability to accept the commonplace injustice of class society.[145]

There was another gap in James' life, caused by his separation from cricket. In the US, he 'never saw a cricket match, though I used to read the results of Tests and county matches which the *New York Times* published every day during the season'. C L R James took only a very superficial interest in the American team sports, which he had never played and were closed to him. He would recall later examples of match-fixing in college basketball and his unhappiness with rude fans at a baseball game.[146] But that was all. He filled the absence of cricket by reading every example of American lowbrow art he could find, magazines, supplements, even children's comics. All such culture, he insisted, did not arise by chance, but reflected deep social processes at work in his adopted country.

Compiled in 1949 and 1950, but only published posthumously, another book, *American Civilisation*, asked what was distinctive about the US. 'The American civilisation is identified in the consciousness of the world with two phases of the development of world history. The first is the Declaration of Independence. The second is mass production.' The former pointed to the past, the latter to the future. 'Liberty, freedom, pursuit of happiness, free individuality had an actuality and meaning in America that they had nowhere else.' How much of this spirit had survived the machine age? 'To sneer' at the American ideology of the free individual, James wrote, would be 'to misunderstand the past of the United States and the tremendous power of this idea which is and will remain a part of the national tradition. *But*, the economic and social structure of the United States has created so huge an apparatus of economic, social and political institutions that the freedom of the individual except in the most abstract terms does not exist.'[147]

At the heart of James' book there are two further, recurring statements. First, America enjoyed an enormously rich popular culture, perhaps the richest such culture the world had known, expressed in cinema, comics, popular journalism, radio serials and mass market-fiction. Second, the American intellectuals had already exhausted any progressive historical role. They 'have nothing to say that is new'. Given their nostalgic hankering for a pre-capitalist past, they were more likely than not to welcome authoritarian forces in the future, whether US or Soviet. James granted a partial, historical exception to but two writers, Walt Whitman and Herman Melville each of whom he showed to be concerned with the central problem of freedom and its preservation in the United States. Neither, however, escaped individualism. While as for the generation of Ernest Hemingway, Richard Wright, Bertram Wolfe and William Faulkner, each one remained 'divorced from any significant current in modern life'.[148] Another book dates from the same period. *Mariners, Renegades and Castaways* is a close reading of Herman Melville's famous novel, *Moby Dick*, which James saw as a prediction of a world in which the science, knowledge and technical ability of mankind would be shown to be incapable of dealing with social crisis. The subject of *Moby Dick* was totalitarian rule. Such things had indeed been created in America during the Civil War. Their experience shaped Melville and still shaped America.[149] The fear of an American totalitarianism was genuine, and widely shared by James' allies.

In 1952, James was arrested for claimed passport violations, and interned on Ellis Island. He was held among Communists, a sure sign to

James that his politics were being misrepresented to the world. He told one correspondent, 'I have heard all sorts of discussions and take part in some that dealt with general matters. But never once have I heard the working class mentioned, either to me or to one another.'[150] C L R James left the United States in 1953, a victim of the long McCarthyite period of repression against the left.

6

Constantine's Influence

(Previous page) The West Indies Test team, June 1963.
Back (l to r): J Solomon, L Gibbs, M Carew, C Griffith, D Murray and B Butcher.
Front (l to r): R Kanhai, C Hunte, F M Worrell, G Sobers and W Hall.

Through the 1950s and 1960s, James failed to settle. London was his usual home, but in 1958 he returned to Trinidad, where he became a leading figure in the national independence movement. Finding disappointment there, James travelled more widely than ever before, revisiting the United States and lecturing in Ghana, where James' former protégé, the post-independence leader Kwame Nkrumah, was for several years an ally. There were also tours of Canada, Cuba, Nigeria, Tanzania and Uganda.

The departure from America in 1953 had a number of consequences. Living in Willesden, James began a third marriage, with New Yorker Selma James.* A supporter of the Johnson-Forest Tendency, with an interest in the labour movement, race questions, and above all the politics of radical feminism, she brought to the marriage a condition of intellectual equality. They were together for ten years. George Lamming's 1972 novel *Natives of My Person* contains two exiled revolutionaries, 'Surgeon' and 'Surgeon's Wife', often said to have been based on the couple. 'He had married her because he needed her support', Lamming wrote, 'but the marriage had gradually withered away.'[151] We can be more prosaic. The marriage seems to have begun in a condition of some euphoria, but was worn down by James' poverty as an occasional public speaker and freelance sporting journalist. Selma worked in the day as a typist, and repeated the role for James in the evenings. When Selma married James she was in her mid-twenties, and such a life may have seemed tolerable to her. It must have been harder for James, who was 30 years her senior.

James' one-time friend and fellow Trinidadian V S Naipaul published after James' death another novel, *A Way in the World*, which contains

---

* Selma James (b. 1930) was a member of the Johnson-Forest Tendency. There, she developed a critique of orthodox Marxism, arguing that Communists and Trotskyists alike had failed to account for the ways in which women's unpaid work is appropriated by capital. After leaving C L R James in the mid-1960s, Selma James was active in women's liberation circles and helped to found the Global Women's Strike campaign.

passages set in 1950s London, at a time when Naipaul was a friend of James. Its author constructs a composite figure, Lebrun, who shares some of James' history: a period in America, the membership of small Marxist groups. He is also in many ways unlike James. Lebrun has a longer period of association with the cause of Trinidadian independence. He is also, crucially, a Stalinist: a device which enables the novelist to portray Lebrun's causes as unequivocally wrong, damned by history and complicit in suffering. The most interesting passages in the book, the ones which best convey the James of the 1950s, and the ones with perhaps the most historical truth, are those that recall the start of the relationship between the narrator and Lebrun, which show an initial sympathy with the older man. 'He was slender and fine-featured: he took care of himself. Close to, he was delicate, smooth-skinned, with a touch of copper in his dark complexion ... He was born to talk. It was as though everything he saw and thought and read was automatically processed into talk material. And it was all immensely intelligent and gripping. He talked about music and the influence on the composers of the instruments of the time. He talked about military matters. I had met no-one like that from our region, no one who had given so much time to reading and thought, no one who had organised so much information in this appetising way. I thought his political reputation simplified the man. And his language was extraordinary ... His spoken sentences, however involved, were complete: they could have been taken down and sent to the printers ... I thought him a prodigy.' V S Naipaul later broke with James, and by the time this novel was published in 2001 was unsympathetic to his former friend. For the sake of completeness, therefore, we should also quote Naipaul's dismissal of Lebrun, 'It was rhetoric, of course.'[152]

James, meanwhile, was trying to regroup the remaining members of the Johnson-Forest Tendency, now just a few dozen in number. In December 1953, he wrote back to Grace Lee, confessing that he could remember almost nothing about his 15 years in America, beyond gramophone records, jazz and films – 'real, ordinary, commonplace movies.'[153]

James' leaving eventually broke up his circle of allies in the US. 'This was partly my fault. I tried to keep leading the party from London, but if I had stayed in the United States we would have had an organisation, because they were good people, trained and full of ability, devoted to the movement. When I left, I told them who should be the leader, and that was blunder number one. That was followed by blunders two, three, four and five.'[154] The worst conflict was between Dunayevskaya and Lee. Dunayevskaya split from James in 1955. While Dunayevskaya, at least as much as James, was committed to the principles of libertarian socialism, it is striking that her later activities were characterised by an organisational discipline that would have made James P Cannon blush. James, meanwhile, was moving in the other direction. His allies formed a looser group, with a journal *Correspondence*. In this new incarnation, the characteristic feature of its work was a sustained, sociological interest in life in the factories and in the working-class home. James' co-thinkers were determined to get away from the clichés of much socialist discourse. The workers were always revolutionary: perhaps, but what were real-life workers actually saying? Such individuals as Charles Denby and Martin Glaberman described life in the auto plants, while others, such as Grace Lee or Selma James, brought the discussion back to the lives of working-class women. The problem of lack of numbers was partly solved by what later revolutionaries would term 'industrialisation': the habit of taking promising students such as Glaberman (a former PhD student) and sending them to work in blue-collar plants. Glaberman was thoroughly principled and remained a revolutionary. The history of the tactic, in other hands, is one of little sustained radicalism and much disappointment.

James also maintained a correspondence with Constance Webb and his son Nobbie. Between 1953 and 1957, he sent back to New York some 30 children's stories for Nobbie, featuring such characters as Nicholas the Worker, Peter the Painter, General Sharkenhower and Moby Dick. Such legends as the Trojan Horse appear in the stories, alongside characters from history, literature and art. There is a political discussion group, the Club, much taken with the demands for collective and personal freedom. Its members discuss freely and reach decisions collectively, and

in several adventures save the world from disaster. The two most important characters are Good Boongko and Bad Boo Boo Loo: their stories
were intended to teach Nobbie right and wrong.[155]

James returned to his previous career in journalism. Once James
was sent to report on a match involving Oxford University. A student
(Naipaul), knowing James, turned to the Oxford Captain: "'Do you
know what the negro is doing?" "Having a day off?" "No, he is reporting the match for the *Manchester Guardian*."'[156] Laughter broke out: the
student acquired a reputation as a joker. But reporting is exactly what
James was doing.

The theme of much of James' cricket writing was the search of individual greatness, as it was a theme also of his previous admiration for
Trotsky. But in his first piece for the *Guardian*, after the end of his 15-year
exile, James struck a different note, arguing that the game had profited
from a series of technical improvements. One he put down to the sheer
numbers of cricketers, the other to an increase also in the number of
cricket journalists. The former had introduced a number of new tech-
niques for playing spin, including 'bringing the left foot forward and
from there watching the ball off the pitch carefully onto the bat'. James
wished the tactic well, ignoring its capacity to encourage defensive play.
James also welcomed the publication of several books on cricket, more
of which had been published in his absence, James guessed, 'than in the
whole previous history of the game'. Journalism opened up the possibility of a democratic relationship between player and crowd. 'Hopes, fears,
jokes (and anger) are shared by players and spectators and through the
highly developed media of mass communication by millions of people
who were formerly excluded. All this makes the game far more interesting to look at than it was.'[157] In 1954, James published some 42 pieces for
the *Guardian*: given the short duration of the cricket season, this meant
two articles a week. Most were simple reports of unexceptional games,
although James was stirred to greater interest by the touring Pakistan
team: including the young leg spinner Khalid Hass.

James was not always happy in this period. The distance from his son must have hurt him deeply. He was isolated from his friends in the US. The old circles of the Pan Africanist movement were not easily reformed: many of the younger generation had now returned to Africa. Many years later the Barbadian author George Lamming would recall meeting James in 1954 by chance on Charing Cross Road, 'James at that time was not in a very good physical condition', Lamming recalls, 'When he said "Lamming" and I said "Yes", I was very excited and a little shocked when he told me who he was.' Lamming also claimed that James liked to spend his days playing pinball in the arcades in Soho.[158]

Yet the possibilities were opening up for renewed agitation. At the start of 1956, Soviet premier Nikita Khrushchev acknowledged publicly that Stalin had committed many 'errors', including the murder of thousands of Communists. Even such a message, glacial in its progress as it may seem to us today, was enough to alarm the British left. The 1956 Congress of the Communist Party of Great Britain made no mention of the secret speech. Previously loyal Communists responded by criticising their leaders, calling for a public discussion to explain why their leaders had never spoken out against Stalin. By the end of the year, British troops were on their way to Egypt, where they were expected to bring an end to the revolt led by the nationalist leader Colonel Nasser. In London's Trafalgar Square vast trade union protests demanded an end to the war. Facing stiff popular resistance, and with the explicit disapproval of the Americans, the British, French and Israeli troops were forced to withdraw. In the aftermath of Suez, Britain was forced to accept the inevitable, and a new policy was adopted of decolonisation. At exactly the same moment that Nasser's victory was being achieved, workers in Budapest were rising with the hope of achieving their independence from the Soviet Union. The most important British eyewitness to the Hungarian events was *Daily Worker* journalist Peter Fryer. When the Communist Party would no longer publish his articles, Fryer joined the Trotskyists instead. Ferment was also rapidly breaking out in the Labour Party, over questions such as nuclear disarmament. James should have been the prophet of the hour. Yet following his disappointment in America, and

ignoring the major organisations of the British left as if they were mori-
bund, James had little influence on the new movement.[159]

James was isolated rather than inactive. In June 1956, workers in
Poland at a ZISPO factory in Poznan went on strike to demand higher
wages. The state responded with repression and 100 workers were killed.
In America, James' allies responded by reproducing a pamphlet from
1950, James, Dunayevskaya and Lee's *State Capitalism and World Revolution*.[160] Nkrumah's party in Ghana won the country's third elections in
July. Other allies were also busy. The next month also saw the publication
of George Padmore's book, *Pan-Africanism or Communism?*, his best-
known work, and a serious attempt to draw the lessons of two decades of
nationalist struggle. In November 1956, following the news of the Budapest uprising, James declared to his allies, 'The news of the last days from
Hungary has come to a climax this morning. We have now seen what, in
my opinion, is the decisive turning point in modern history. The first was
the Paris revolution of 1848; the second was the Commune; the third
was the Russian October Revolution. This Hungarian revolution is the
last, and incomparably the greatest of them all.'[161] With *State Capitalism*
already at the printers, James' comrades were able only to add just a few
words to the back cover on the subject of the Hungarian revolt.

The highpoint of the Hungarian revolution came at the end of
October 1956, when a parliament of workers' councils was elected. It
declared: 'The supreme controlling body of the factory is the workers'
council democratically elected by the workers ... The director is employed
by the factory. The director and highest employees are to be elected by
the workers' council ... the director is responsible to the workers' council
in every matter.'[162] When James' considered response to the events of
1956 appeared, it was in a new book, *Facing Reality*. The message of
Hungary, James argued, was that workers' power was already a reality.
'The socialist society exists' on the shop floor, it just 'has to get rid of
what is stifling it, what is preventing it from expanding to the full, what is
preventing it from tackling not only the immediate problem of production, but also the more general problems of society'.[163] Socialism already

existed in the factories. It only needed to announce itself. Such passages are strikingly similar to some of James' contemporary statements on the maturity of the African revolution. The depressing reality, however, is that the Hungarian uprising failed to spread, and was crushed within weeks. The first workers' councils were established on 23 October; the Soviet attack began on 4 November. The workers called a general strike, but by the end of the year, they had been defeated. In England, James complained, the cause of Hungary was taken up by the anti-Communist right, 'thousands of dyed-in-the-wool conservatives found themselves urging on and cheering the rebellion led by Hungarian workers under the leadership of workers' councils against a totalitarian government'.[164] There was a non-Stalinist left in the process of being born, but James had no links to it, and was in no position to influence the former Communists who dominated it. Indeed if he was heard in Britain at all, it was through a very small number of loyal James-ians emerging from other Trotskyist parties,[165] or through student followers of the *Universities and Left Review*, whose writers including Stuart Hall were in flux between Labourist and later Marxist positions.

Of all James' campaigns following his return from America, none gave him greater opportunities than events in Trinidad and Tobago. The British hold weakened when a series of labour disputes, including the oil-workers' strike of 1937,[166] began to challenge the remaining structures of imperial rule. A number of reforms were made, which opened up such careers as education and the civil service. By 1954, James' former student from the 1920s, Eric Williams, was working for the Caribbean Commission, a British-run project to investigate the condition of the islands, and to advocate further reform. The Commission was equally intended to block proposals for independence.

Williams' relationship with James had lasted for three decades. In the 1940s, Williams' history of the relationship between *Capitalism and Slavery* had vindicated the old Marxist claim that the condition for Western prosperity had been the profits of the slave trade. Williams even sent a copy of the book to James, inscribed 'Dear Jimmy. Your godchild!'

James in turn had long spoken highly of Williams, telling Constance Webb in 1944, 'I have a son you know. He is thirty years old. I watch over him like a trainer and prize-fighter. Of course he is not my son really. He is a young West Indian, a scholar of repute ... For nearly 12 years now I have watched him come along. He is sometimes very thoughtless and selfish. But I don't mind. Seeing him develop pleases me.'[167] In a later manuscript, James would describe how he had used to watch over Williams in London: 'I am quite a cautious man and on quite a few evenings Williams and his friends went pub crawling, accompanied by me with Marx, Jane Austen, or H. G. Wells in my pockets, which I faithfully read during the pauses. At the end I got into a cab with Williams and saw him safely home to my flat.'[168] Perhaps James was more like a young uncle than a father.

Events in Trinidad were moving rapidly. Williams left the Caribbean Commission in 1954, setting out his grievances in a series of public talks, the largest of which in the Trinidad Public Library was attended by 700 people, with many outside, hearing the proceedings relayed by loudspeaker. Sensing the birth of a mass, popular support, Williams founded the People's National Movement (PNM). Williams then toured Trinidad, arguing for the creation of a genuine West Indian federal democracy, the first stage towards self-government. The PNM won elections in 1956, becoming the dominant force in Trinidad and Tobago, a position it retained for three decades. By 1958, Williams was Prime Minister. In 1956, Williams took the first draft of the *People's Charter,* the founding document of the PNM, to London where James read and commented upon it. Following independence, Learie Constantine returned to Trinidad, where he joined Williams' cabinet.[169] Eric Williams then invited James to follow Constantine.

With Williams' backing, James became the editor of the *PNM Weekly* (later *The Nation*), the party newspaper. One writer, Basil Wilson, portrays James as taking this position in full consciousness of the gap between his own politics and Williams'. 'When James returned to the Caribbean, he did so without any romantic illusions about establishing a revolutionary society. He returned to the Caribbean willing to abandon temporarily his own revolutionary activities and to work sacrificially for the building of the People's National Movement into a mass force. Here, one has to pause, catch a few gasps, and ponder awhile. Now this was truly the act of a remarkable man. Convinced that this was where the mass movement in Trinidad was at this historical juncture, C L R James buried his revolutionary Marxist position, not to lead the nationalist struggle but to edit the PNM paper and to do the nitty-gritty unglamorous, organisational tasks most theoreticians simply shun.'[170] There may be some romanticising in Wilson's account. Control of a newspaper was a definite form of authority, and, yes, even of leadership. It was also one ideally suited to James' great talent as a writer.

Although James returned to Trinidad at Williams' prompting, it seems that the younger man was unprepared for his presence, disliked the realisation that he now had a potential critic to his left, and did little of significance to help James find his feet. In March 1960, James sent a 40,000-word statement to the PNM representative on the paper's Board of Directors. It was an attempt to draw the lessons of his work on the paper. James complained of 'the almost total absence of any official interest by the Party' in the paper. He had been required to find the machinery to print the paper by scavenging from junk heaps. The paper had been a success, but no thanks to the government, which had simply refused to provide any financial or other support. 'In all my experience I have never known or heard of any paper, least of all an official organ, which in editorial range and point, production, advertisements, circulation, starting with a grossly incompetent accountant, a disloyal assistant, an office boy, a borrowed typewriter, one filing cabinet and one desk, has reached where *The Nation* has reached in fifteen months, with the political and other journalistic prestige of the paper of an international scale … a circulation of 12,000 and the respect and the confidence of a large majority of the population.'[171]

There was one campaign in which James was allowed to use the full force of his energy, his drive to secure for Frank Worrell the captaincy of the West Indies' cricket team. Worrell's chief rival, F C S Alexander, kept wicket for the team. He was a good batsman, James insisted, and a real fighter. Yet Worrell, he wrote, 'is at the peak of his reputation not only as a cricketer but as a master of the game'. Others have gone further. Worrell, according to one US critic, was 'a cultivated gentleman, a product of Combermere, Barbados' finest public school; a graduate of Manchester University; the leading batsman in the West Indies; and ranked among the top four or five batsmen in the world. While these credentials argued strongly in his favour, they were all overruled by the fact of his colour.'[172] James refrained from arguing for Worrell, and against Alexander, on colour alone. Yet everyone knew that this was the heart of the dispute. For Worrell was black, Alexander white, and the West Indies had never yet had a black captain. Among the white population of the West Indies, there was resistance to James' campaign. When England toured the islands in 1959–60, the white players in the West Indies team invited the English tourists to their homes for cocktails; they pointedly did not invite their black team-mates. The writer E W Swanton accompanied the English players. He supported James' campaign, for the reason that Frank Worrell seemed to him to be a better player and probably a better captain. Swanton was also struck by the effect James had had in polarising opinion: 'This is a cricket book, not a treatise on West Indian problems, but these was one aspect of current life in the islands which I noticed more this time, in relation to the cricket than on previous visits, and I must mention it though, I hope, with due diffidence. I mean the matter of colour prejudice.'[173] For once, Williams backed James, and Worrell triumphed in 1960.

Such modest victories aside, the new Trinidadian state failed to live up to its early promise and soon James was disenchanted. Like many of the leaders of the first wave of independent states, Eric Williams began with a commitment to equality, but lacked any strong sense of how to achieve it. In a world economy that remained capitalist, any small state was likely to depend on largesse from the rich powers. One year's loan became next year's debt. The post-independence leadership lost its organic links to people in struggle, and increasingly saw them as a barrier to its own advance.

In late 1959, James wrote to one correspondent, complaining of the breakdown in intra-party relationships: 'The situation is bad. I don't believe the participants all know how bad it is. It is a situation where it appears to be all suspicion, misunderstanding, tactlessness, jealousies, immaturity, etc., on the surface. The persistence of these and the inability to overcome them point, in my opinion, to serious political differences, of which the persons involved or some of them, are only vaguely but substantially aware. If there is "immaturity", it is only in the fact that there is no urgent attempt at clarification. The result is that suspicions grow and tensions increase.'[174]

By early 1960, James was writing to Williams, arguing that the PNM should be transformed into a democratic organisation. 'The party does not merely convey the ideas, actions and projects of the political leadership. It does not merely transform these ideas into shapes and languages that the people are able to absorb. A mass party of this kind is the sole means by which the developing consciousness of the people can be translated into such forms as to make the people conscious of what it is they want, of the possibilities and limitations of their desires.'[175] In a letter from March 1960, James went further: 'A crisis has developed between *The Nation* and the Party. The consequences of this are likely to be felt throughout the West Indies and abroad.' His solution: '1) The Party is to separate itself from the Government to live an independent life. 2) The Party is represented in the Government by the Cabinet and the Ministers. 3) The Party must have its own "Cabinet" and its own "Ministers" in the National office, centering around the Secretary, the Editor of the Party Newspaper, the Organiser.'[176]

Arguments over organisation acted as a proxy for disputes as to the political direction the PNM should take. One disagreement between C L R James and Williams concerned the latter's decision to allow the American Navy to retain a base at Chaguaramas on the islands. It was an argument that had been raised first by Williams himself, back in 1957, and no one then had been firmer in arguing that the land belonged to Trinidad and not to America. As late as April 1960, he led large protests soon known as the 'March in the Rain' to the United States consulate, where demands for the return of the base were read to officials. Over the subsequent months, events moved quickly. Britain agreed to independence for the West Indies, America agreed to recognise the government of Trinidad, and Williams dropped his demands for Chaguaramas.

In the midst of this argument, James published a pamphlet, *A Convention Appraisal*, sketching Eric Williams' career for members of his party. 'Dr. Williams,' James wrote, 'is a post-war nationalist politician in an underdeveloped colonial territory which is still not independent.' He described Williams' vital role in founding the PNM, and enabling the movement for independence to take shape. James reported Williams' many academic victories. He portrayed his friend as a national leader, 'in every sense as complete a West Indian citizen as it is possible to be today.'[177] He spoke of the need for the PNM to become a proper party, like the People's National Party in Jamaica, Labour in Britain, or the Conservatives. He nowhere puffed Williams up. He nowhere presented Williams as being radical on any question save the national one.

By the end of the summer, James had been frozen out of discussions within the PNM. He was not consulted as to the decision over Chaguaramas. He felt he had no choice but to resign as editor of his paper. 'I see no future,' James wrote, for the paper, 'unless it is linked to the Party and a reorganised Party, because to link it to the present Party is not only useless but impossible.' Williams was turning sharply to the right. In summer 1960, Williams told his listeners that 'if the world were divided into two camps, the West Indies which was historically, geographically and economically in the Western Hemisphere, could not claim it was going to be in the middle. If the Communists and fellow travellers were counting on him to pull their chestnuts out of the fire they would be disappointed.'[178]

In winter and spring 1960/1, James found himself under attack from his erstwhile comrades in the PNM. The Central Executive bought various charges against him, accusing James of accepting bribes, and of having published various documents inimical to the Movement. James was ordered to attend a disciplinary committee hearing on 24 March 1961.[179] James showed all the charges against him to be false, but was expelled from the party. Despite this defeat, James remained in Trinidad. He seems to have gone through moments of real hope as well as periods of despair. Following his expulsion at the end of March, James told one correspondent: 'While the mass of the public, though uncertain, is more or less following along, a substantial layer of intelligent and extremely active people in the party and the young people in particular feel that they have been sold out ... It is equally recognised that for the first time in the island there is someone who is perfectly able to take care of Williams in debate, public authority and political competence. That person is myself.'[180]

Around this time James published a book, *Modern Politics*, providing an optimistic account of 'the ascent to man of complete humanity', beginning with Greek notions of democracy, rising through Marx and Rousseau to the democratic opportunities of the post-war world: 'Properly encouraged and given a sense of history and a sense of destiny [people] will do all they now do for war, for the sake of improving the normal life and relations of human beings. But this will only come when people are their own masters.'[181] Another book, *Party Politics in the West Indies*, concentrated on explaining the rift with Williams. In 1965, James also helped to found the Workers and Farmers Party, to protest against the degeneration of the independence movement, and to express the contrast between the official leadership of the Caribbean and what he insisted was 'the deep democratic instincts of our population'. Yet the Workers and Farmers Party was defeated in the 1966 elections, with James winning just 2.8 per cent of the vote in Tunapuna. Only later would his allies reassert themselves in campaigns such as the Oilfield Workers' Trade Union, led by James' friend George Weekes.[182]

As the government found a new social base among those who already had a stake in the system, James had the partial recompense of watching the success of his brother Eric. 'My brother never played any games to speak of, but as a young man he gave some clerical assistance to the secretary of the local Football Association. In time became the secretary.'[183] Three years C L R's junior, Eric had begun work as a railway clerk in 1921. He was able to rise up the ladder, becoming a Railway Accountant and Secretary of the Trinidad Amateur Football Association in his forties. In 1961, just months after C L R was removed from the PNM, his brother was appointed General Manager of the Government Railway. Two years' later, he was awarded a one-off payment by the Football Association of $12,000, generous enough to be widely covered in the local press. Ambitious, often seen as aloof, Eric was better suited to success under the Williams' regime.

It was in Trinidad that James also completed the writing of his famous 1963 work, *Beyond a Boundary*, a remarkable text, written in strong, rhythmic prose and with a substantial autobiographical element. In it C L R James demonstrates that cricket could work both to reinforce British colonial rule, and as a site of resistance. James develops this dual argument through a study of the lives of the inter-war West Indian cricketers, including George John, Wilton St Hill, Percy Tarilton and George Challenor. We can describe the structure of the book briefly. We have already cited the two anecdotes with which *Beyond a Boundary* opens, concerning Bondman and Jones. James treats these memories as the starting points of a connected pattern: 'Hegel says somewhere that the old man repeats the prayers he repeated as a child, but now with the experience of a lifetime. Here briefly are some of the experiences of a lifetime, which have placed Matthew Bondman and Arthur Jones within a frame of reference that stretches east and west into the receding distance, back into the past and forward into the future.'[184] James shows the influence on him, as of any West Indian of his generation, of English literature, cricket and religion. By cricket, James makes clear he means the customs surrounding the game, not just the sport itself. In the inter-war West Indies, James argues, sporting rivalries drove conflicts of race and class, which would soon be expressed politically. Returning to Britain,

James contends, the imperial ruling class chose the public schools to equip themselves with an ideology. At the heart of its message was self-restraint. In Britain, cricket served to unify a class. The sport was then exported to the Caribbean. Towards the end of his book, James criticises the habits of modern cricket, its professionalisation and its rejection of risks. These choices, James portrays as the corollary of a welfare society and the triumph of the bureaucratic instinct in Europe.

Along the way, *Beyond a Boundary* pays off several long-standing debts of gratitude. The first is to the English public school system, which James does by means of an extended anecdote. James describes watching Labour politician Nye Bevan address a Manchester audience in 1956, in the months before Hungary and Suez, and at a time when Bevan was allowing his name to be attached to the demand for nuclear disarmament. The London press criticised him for 'not playing with the team'. Bevan bit back. Why should he keep a stiff upper lip or play with a straight bat? Those were the terms not of the working class but of the middle class, not of the trade unions but of the English public schools. 'I smiled too,' James recalls, 'but not whole-heartedly. In the midst of his fireworks Mr. Bevan had dropped a single sentence that tolled like a bell. "I did not join the Labour Party, I was brought up in it." Not C L R James, of course, for I had been brought up in the public-school code.'[185]

James's youth had been spent in reading and on cricket. Those habits were part of his personality before his scholarship. His teachers only developed and made coherent what was already there. To join these two points, and draw them into a triangle, *Beyond a Boundary* identifies a third process: puritanism. The essence of the social code of cricket, James explains, was self-restraint. A good cricketer, James had been taught, was one who batted and bowled honestly, and one above all who never questioned the decisions of the umpire. *Beyond a Boundary* explains James' life-long admiration for Thackeray in very similar terms. 'In recent years, as I have re-read Thackeray, I see the things which I did not in the early years. I took them for granted, and they were therefore all the more effective … the British discipline, the stiff lips, upper and lower. When Major

Dobbin returns from India, and he and Amelia greet each other, Thackeray asks: why did Dobbin not speak? Not only Dobbin, it is Thackeray who does not speak.'[186] Neither did James, if we recall Webb's complaints through the demise of their marriage.

In another striking passage, James apologises to the English for having accused them once of lacking any culture. In his book on Cipriani, he acknowledges that he had once written, 'If anyone happens to meet fairly frequently any group of Englishmen, even of university education, he will find as a rule that they dislike civilised conversation and look with suspicion, if not positive dislike, upon anyone who introduces it into their continual reverberations over the football match, the cricket match, the hockey match or the tennis match. How often one meets an Englishman, who though not a sportsman, tries to make it appear as if he is or has been one.'[187] In *Beyond a Boundary*, James accepts that sport is a mighty part of world culture, and therefore that football and cricket represented the real and lasting English gift.

You could take James' analysis and phrase it not as an argument but as a question and in pseudo-Marxist terms. If most people spend their lives at work, in miserable and alienated conditions, then on leaving work why do so many choose sport for their escape? Perhaps unfairly on Trotsky, James paraphrases his former teacher as arguing that workers were deflected from politics by their interest in sport. 'With my past, I simply could not accept that.'[188] 'Cricket is first and foremost a dramatic spectacle,' James writes: 'It belongs with the theatre, ballet, opera and dance.' Cricket's specific character, *Beyond a Boundary* argues, is two-fold. First, it pits two characters, the batsman and the bowler, in competition with each other. 'The batsman facing the ball does not merely represent his side. For that moment, to all intents and purposes, he is his side.' Secondly, a cricket match, as a result often of its long duration, tends to alternate moments of long calm with sudden energy. 'Within the fluctuating interest of the rise or fall of the game as a whole, there is this unending series of events, each single one fraught with immense possibilities of expectation and realisation.' Cricket is a constant, artistic spectacle.[189]

James portrays cricket as a pre-capitalist sport which was appropriated by the Victorian bourgeoisie. He begins with Thomas Arnold, the 19th-century headmaster of Rugby School. Arnold saw his task as being to inculcate not learning but character. The testament to Arnold's system was Thomas Hughes' novel *Tom Brown's Schooldays*. None of the characters shows much talent as students. That was never the point of the system. Tom's ascendancy is based on his prowess as a runner, footballer and crucially as a cricketer. Long before cricket had been able to play its later role as the sport of empire, schoolboys were educated into the moral values of the game. Nine years after Hughes' book, the player emerged who would express its values to a national audience: W G Grace. 'W. G.'s batting figures, remarkable as they are, lose all their true significance unless they are seen in close relations with the history of cricket itself and the social history of England. Unless you do this you fall head foremost into the trap of making comparisons with [Donald] Bradman. Bradman piled up centuries, W. G. built a social organisation.'[190]

Beyond a Boundary is dedicated to three men, W G Grace, Learie Constantine and Frank Worrell. The choice of Grace may appear surprising, but one recurring aspect of the book is its author's admiration for the British way of life that James finds embodied in the game. James' proof of the stature of Grace comes from the results of the annual match between amateur and professional, 'Gentlemen' versus 'Players'. Before Grace and after, this match was always an easy victory for the professionals. Yet in Grace's days, a different spirit was at its height. In this story, James was with Grace. 'Grace won the matches for the Gentlemen. We need not give the figures. He not only smashed what had been the Players' greatest strength, fast bowling. He so established the morale of the Gentlemen that though the Players recovered, it was many years before it was possible to look upon the Players as the more likely winners ... Gentlemen would not have continued to win the Battle of Waterloo if they had continued to meet annual Waterloos at Lord and the Oval.' James rises to heights of hyperbole: 'No crusader was more suited to his time than was W.G. to his own; none rendered more service to the world

... He had enriched the depleted lives of two generations and millions yet to be born. He had extended our conception of human capacity and in doing all this he had done no harm to anyone.'[191]

James' argument can be summarised as follows. Cricket was originally the sport of pre-industrial England. The public schools opened up the possibility of some new order. Under Grace's influence, this prospect was duly achieved. Cricket established a mass audience, not especially in London but all over England. 'Never since the days of the Olympic champions of Greece has the sporting world known such enthusiasm and never since.' Another chapter, titled (with a bow to Spengler) *Decline of the West*, then describes the demise of cricket after 1914, in tune with the decline of British imperial ambition. Bodyline was the key episode, as an English cricket team incapable of maintaining its hegemony through talent or influence turned to violence, shredding the vestigial promise of the public school morality. Decline continued through the 1950s. We cited earlier an article from 1953, in which James had observed a tendency towards the more defensive playing of spin. Such cricketers as Cowdrey, Graveney and May, had become overly pre-occupied with the defence, James insisted. 'These are the Welfare Staters,' he wrote.[192]

So from where was cricket supposed to renew itself? 'C L R James', writes Francis Wheen, 'was a romantic traditionalist. The heroes of *Beyond a Boundary* were Thomas Arnold, the 19th-century headmaster of Rugby, Thomas Hughes, the author of *Tom Brown's Schooldays* and W. G. Grace. James was dazzled by the "grandeur" and "moral revelation" of Arnold's ideas, apparently happy to overlook the fact that these ideas included a contempt for the working class and a terror of universal suffrage.'[193] It would follow that James' solutions were backward looking. They were not. Wheen is only half right, and he has chosen the least interesting half of the argument. What James discovered in W G Grace was a freedom of constraint, a rejection of the market, which James also found expressed in the cricket of the West Indies, and found there in a higher form.

Much turns, then, on James' treatment of Learie Constantine. For

Constantine was the star of the West Indies tours of England in the 1920s and 1930s. Chosen to represent the West Indies on a tour of England in 1923, Constantine excelled as a fielder. We have given some examples already of his talent in the covers. He was at this time though a player of greater promise than achievement. James tells a story of Constantine in 1926, which conveys the quality of his performances of the time. Batting against Wally Hammond, Constantine was surprised by a ball pitched wide outside his off stump and turning back sharply towards him. 'Doubling himself almost in two, to give himself space, he cut the ball a little to the left of point for a four which no one in the world, not even himself, could have stopped ... What made us sit up and take notice was that he had never in his life made such a stroke before, that came out afterwards, and he had had no premeditated idea of making any such stroke. I do not remember seeing it again.'[194] In 1928, the West Indies played again in England, and Constantine achieved the double of 100 wickets and 100 runs. He had finally arrived.

Beyond a Boundary makes two profound observations about Constantine's success. First, James argues that Constantine's professional success was not made in the West Indies but in England. It depended largely on the character not of Test, nor even first-class but of league cricket. Recall, this was the era before television, when the only real way to see the stars was in the flesh. League cricket was a more localised version of the game, capable of being watched not by thousands but by hundreds of thousands of people each year. As Grace had established a first-class circuit, so Constantine's personality won an audience for the leagues. Note also that league cricket, unlike its first-class counterpart, was a single innings game. Constantine's style in this setting, James argues, was to bat in a way that was both orthodox and dissident: first he would settle, next he would score around the ground, until the field was widely set. Then he would accumulate patiently. Nothing was left to chance, but to talent and the habit of success.

Secondly, James treats his friend not as an individual but as the representative of a generation. He was the first West Indian player to prove to the world the talent in the islands. We need to recall the context, to remember that the West Indies' games against an MCC tour in 1923 were the first that had been granted even first-class status. We should recall also that the 1928 matches in which Constantine played were the first official Tests between the West Indies and England. 'Constantine wanted to use his great reputation in order to clear a road for others. He knew their difficulties, which his special gifts had enabled him to overcome.' The West Indies' defeat of England at Georgetown in 1930 was their first victory. Constantine took nine wickets in the game, for 122 runs. There was a buzz about Caribbean cricket, which he both helped to begin and incarnated. Learie Constantine was an immensely popular player. Whenever he was chosen, the crowds appeared. He could play this role, James argues, because an audience of British workers treated him as a harbinger. He was the sign first that West Indies' cricket could now match England's. He was a sign also of the coming demand for colonial freedom, for a thoroughgoing equality between black and white. 'All that we did, thought and hoped for ... was carried to the heights by Constantine.'[195]

James also treats Constantine's understanding of the politics of race as having been consistently in advance of his own. We can recall his friend's words that James found so troubling in 1923, 'They are no better than we.' We can recall also the contrast between James' long identification with the ethics of cricket, and Constantine's scepticism of the 'gospel of true sportsmanship', as well as Constantine's consistent involvement in British politics. In 1954, Constantine published his famous book *Colour Bar*, a denunciation of the racism he had experienced in Britain, and all the more powerful because of his own position as a sporting celebrity: 'I have been refused food in a London restaurant', Constantine wrote, 'and submitted to ignominy when I asked for rooms in a London hotel.' Nor were the experiences his alone, 'A few weeks ago, an old friend went to a Roman Catholic church near Paddington in London where his baby was to be baptised. According to the listed arrangements, this baby was to be the fourth of a number present to go through the ceremony. But when the baby's godmother advanced in her place, the priest held out a warning hand, shook his head and whispered: "Please wait!" ... She was publicly held back until all nine white babies had been baptised, though the others arrived long after. Finally, the little black child was allowed to come to Jesus who said on another occasion when his disciples intervened with their ideas, "Suffer little children.""[196]

Constantine's last public campaign in Britain took place in 1964 as High Commissioner of Trinidad and Tobago. Hearing of the iron rule which banned black people from working on Bristol's buses, Constantine denounced the racism of the employers. But this was to interfere in the politics of another country, and Eric Williams insisted that Constantine had to resign. 'Suffice it to say that among other things my government felt I had exceeded my duties during the Bristol affair and should have recognised it as an internal matter for Management and Union.'[197]

In stressing Constantine's influence, James was perhaps too modest about his own contribution. James was not the first black writer to describe racism. Yet while Constantine and others could describe racism only as a repeated experience felt by individuals, James' developed a language to connect together the experiences.

In a separate interview, Constantine once stated that he lacked James' belief in cricket as morality, telling Chris Searle that 'cricket is the most obvious and some would say glaring example of the black man being kept "in his place"'.[198] Such an argument is never put in *Beyond a Boundary*, but is surely one point to which the argument is always tending. Cricket can be the means by which racial hierarchies are reinforced, or one means by which they can be overthrown. Derek Walcott claims rightly that '*Beyond a Boundary* can be thought of as a subversion; it undermines concepts that feel safe ... its technique is not bitterness but joy'.[199] Analysis founding in the deep grammar of cricket is always going further, so that the book becomes not the world seen through cricketing eyes, but the nature of the world against the de-politicised self-image of the game.

The book's final hero is Frank Worrell, the first black captain of the

West Indies, and the man responsible for the victorious West Indies tour of Australia in 1960. 'Worrell is one of the few who after a few hours of talk have left me as tired as if I had been put through a wringer. His responses to difficult questions were so unhesitating, so precise, and so took the subject onto unsuspected but relevant areas, that I felt it was I who was undergoing examination. No cricketer, and I have talked to many, ever shook me up in a similar fashion ... What I am dealing with here is a unique capacity to concentrate all the forces available and for the matter in hand.' Worrell was fortunate in the players he led, including above all Garfield Sobers. 'For years I have believed,' James continues, 'that Sobers was the greatest of living batsmen.' Elsewhere James described him as the 'living embodiment of centuries of a tortured history'.[200] Sobers was also an all-rounder, equally devastating in his twenties as a pace bowler, and later with swing and even spin.

Why was James such a consistent admirer of cricketers such as Constantine or Sobers who could both bat and bowl? One answer is provided not in *Beyond a Boundary*, but in a separate and later piece written by James' fellow cricketing Marxist, Paul Foot. 'Such players invariably upset specialists, commentators and authorities. The reason is that they are, literally, carefree when they bat and bowl. When a specialist batsman fails, a little nick at the ball just outside the off stump, his very livelihood is in jeopardy. The same fate threatens a specialist bowler when he fails to get that little nick, and ends up with nought for sixty in twenty overs. But the all-rounder bats and bowl knowing that of he fails, he can redeem his failure in the other role. So it is that, for the fanatics as well, the great all-rounders are the greatest gifts to an already gift-laden game.'[201]

Frank Worrell and Garfield Sobers' greatness found a sporting expression. The 1961 West Indies tour of Australia, James concludes, saw cricket of an unparalleled quality. The West Indies lost, but both they and Richie Benaud's Australia played at an extraordinary tempo. When the Caribbean team left the country, half a million Australians turned out to bid them farewell. 'The West Indies team in Australia on the field and off was playing above what it knew of itself. What they discovered in themselves must have been a revelation to few more than to the players themselves ... The first innings of Sobers at Brisbane was the most beautiful batting I have ever seen. Never was such ease and certainty of stroke, such early seeing of the ball, such late and leisured play, such command by the batsman not only of the bowling but of himself.' James' verdict conveys the sense of the historical importance he found in the 1961 tour. Their cricket was revolution. It was history: 'It was simply a return to the batting of the Golden Age.'[202]

7

Ghana: Defeat Again

(Previous page) President Kwame Nkrumah of Ghana *(centre)*, 1962.

On his return from Trinidad in 1963, James settled again in London. Jim Higgins was a friend in this period, 'One of the things I remember about him is the gesture he used to make when he had brought his argument to a suitable conclusion. He would strike his hands together as if he were playing the cymbals and would produce his final words in cadence with the up-and-down hand movements. It was a pretty effective way of lending weight and significance to his words. On one occasion my wife and baby daughter went to tea in the garden in Staverton Road. We sat out in the sunshine, chatting and being suitably impressed with my infant child. Selma bought out some chocolate biscuits and offered the tin to the baby Judith. She had never been allowed free access to biscuit tins before and dived in, emerging with a biscuit in each hand. My wife remonstrated with her but Nello intervened saying "No, no, under socialism every baby will have a chocolate biscuit in each hand", accompanying this with his silent cymbal routine.'[203]

In June 1967, James attended a conference on workers' control in Hull. The British social historian Edward Thompson was at the podium, and responding to James' question from the floor, he used the opportunity to applaud his fellow activist: 'When one looks back over the last twenty years to those men who are most far-sighted, who first began to tease out the muddle of ideology in our times, who were at the same time Marxist with a hard theoretical basis, and close students of society, humanists with a tremendous response to, and understanding of human culture, Comrade James is one of the first one thinks of.'[204]

For James, London was a base from which to maintain alliances in several countries. The setback in Trinidad did not bring an end to James' involvement in post-colonial politics. James had met several of the leaders of the later African independent states. We have already seen James' earlier view that socialism and black liberation represented a joint cause. By the 1960s, that equivalence no longer seems to be James' true opinion. He related to the Trotskyist tradition in a critical manner, while tending to minimise the problems facing the movements of the Third World. Again and again, James accused the Trotskyists of wrongly idealising state planning, and by implication giving an exaggerated role in history to the middle classes, at the expense of workers. But read James on the role of African writers, and attack has been transformed into defence. In Africa, he insisted, planning was required. In Africa, the intellectual should lead. 'The man at the helm is the African intellectual. He succeeds, or independent Africa sinks. Yet Western racial prejudice is so much a part of the Western outlook on life that the African intellectual continues to be looked upon as some kind of primitive barbarian climbing the sharp and slipper slope to civilisation.'[205]

A talk from 1969 made much the same point. Reflecting on news of the revolution in Tanzania, C L R James said, 'It is when the combination is made between the obscure local figures and the masses of the population and the intellectuals, those who can teach the whole and express themselves to a general public, then something is really revolutionary. Until that time you have revolutionary actions; you have revolutionary intent; but you haven't got a revolution positive, a general revolutionary programme.'[206] How can this idealisation of the African intellectual be squared with James contempt for the Western intellectual in *American Civilisation*? If the answer is that James thought different historical tasks were open to Africa and Europe, then how was that message different from the idea of socialism by stages (first national liberation and only later socialism) for which he had once excoriated the Western Communists?

James was surprisingly poorly equipped for the betrayal of post-colonial societies by their leaders. The pattern set by Williams in Trinidad was to repeat itself. In the 1950s, James hailed Nkrumah as 'Africa's Lenin', only to see his regime destroyed by a military coup. After Nkrumah, James gave his praise to Tanzania's Nyerere, 'the highest peak reached so far by revolting blacks', before later breaking with Nyerere too.[207]

More positively, James also influenced the second generation of African liberation struggles of the 1970s. While the independence campaigns of the early 1950s and 1960s engaged with Russian models, the campaigns of the 1970s were more militant. For good and for ill, the

China of the Cultural Revolution had a greater influence. James was both a radicalising and at times a calming influence on such outstanding revolutionaries as Walter Rodney, the Guyanese Marxist, murdered by his state in 1980.[208]

Understanding James' relationship to Kwame Nkrumah* is crucial to making sense of this period of his life. Between 1935 and 1945, Nkrumah was living in the US, where he came to hear of the International African Service Bureau and met James in New York in 1941. Two years later, he announced that he would be moving to London, and asked James for a letter of recommendation to Padmore. James believed that Nkrumah's head was full of Stalinist cliché, and his letter to Padmore described Nkrumah as determined but 'not very bright' (a judgment that caused James some modest embarrassment later).[209] Nkrumah returned to the Gold Coast in December 1947. In Accra, he founded the Convention People's Party, which won a clear majority of seats in the country's first democratic elections. The British Governor invited Nkrumah to head a government, and to lead the country to independence. In 1952, upon the withdrawal of the British, Nkrumah was appointed Prime Minister. When Ghana achieved independence in 1958 Nkrumah became the country's first President. James met Nkrumah in Accra in 1957, telling him that the revolt of the people of Ghana was 'one of the most significant revolutions of the century ... He said he had been thinking the same.'[210]

Nkrumah was now widely seen as a leader of global stature, alongside the likes of Nasser, Nehru and Castro. Padmore worked for Nkrumah until his death in 1959, and the veteran American socialist W E B

---

* Kwame Nkrumah (1909–72) was born at Nkroful in what was then the British colonial territory of the Gold Coast. Nkrumah was a student at Lincoln University in Pennsylvania when met James. Arriving in London in 1945 he came into contact with George Padmore, with whom he helped to organise the Sixth Pan-African Congress in Manchester. He was later the first post-independence leader of Ghana. Overthrown by a Western-backed coup, he spent his last years in exile in Romania.

DuBois also came to live in Ghana. Yet for years Nkrumah's position faced challenges. Rival factions abounded, while Nkrumah responded to criticism in a high-handed manner. Dissidents were jailed. Trade union critics were silenced by granting them positions of authority, which they misused as opportunities for graft. Those who refused to be co-opted were jailed. Between 1957 and 1960, Nkrumah attempted to ally with the British and American powers. Later, he tacked left. Neither move had the unambiguous support of the majority in the country. In 1960, James visited Ghana, and learned from friends of an all-pervasive spirit of corruption. He gave a speech to Nkrumah's supporters that warmly praises his friend but also contained a coded warning of the dangers of proceeding along a radical path without popular support. Nkrumah told James that he would publish the speech, but in James' absence, he chose not to do so.[211]

If Nkrumah took James' advice it was in the opposite direction to the one meant: promises of support for other liberation movements were shelved, the regime went on with the business of accumulation. In the Congo, where a Belgian-sponsored civil war culminated in the murder of the elected president Patrice Lumumba, Nkrumah emerged as the chief architect of a United Nations intervention, which delivered the country (ultimately) into the hands of her generals. Over Vietnam, Nkrumah supported moves to establish a Commonwealth contingent in support of the American war.[212]

In December 1963, following a botched assassination attempt on Nkrumah, James wrote privately to his friend, expressing at last his doubts: 'This is a terrible business, bound to have effects far outside Ghana and in Ghana itself. I shall have to speak and write about it, people, not enemies, already are asking me along these lines, "Well, James, what have you to say?" But I will not say anything until I know what you have to say ... What I am concerned about it is the impact that Ghana and you are making on the world and on Africa ... I hope, my dear

Francis,* you have people around to tell you quite plainly what is now required from you. It is quite possible that this unfortunate happening can be turned into a positive stage in the evolution of Ghana, all Africa and in fact governments everywhere. If there is anything you think I can do, you know that I am at your service.[213]

A month later, James made his letter public. 'I suppose it brings to an end an association of twenty years that I have valued more than most ... Nkrumah did not need my support. I needed his. I have been and am concerned with and active in a lot of politics, one part of which was and is the expulsion of imperialism from Africa and the development of underdeveloped countries. In the expulsion of imperialism from Africa, a small group of us have been remarkably successful ... Nkrumah played a great role; he is one of the greatest of living politicians ... When people pointed out what they considered negative aspects of his régime I held my peace because I knew the positive aspects, the immense positive aspects. But when he was shot at a second time, I wrote to him hinting that something was wrong with his régime, which demanded certain attention, otherwise people don't shoot.'[214]

James' thought-out reflections on Nkrumah appeared after Nkrumah's defeat, in his 1977 book, *Nkrumah and the Ghana Revolution* (most of the chapters had been written in 1957, but a preface brought the argument up to date). In this book, James maintained that 'elements of colonialism still lurk in the minds even of independent countries'. He was convinced that any successful independence movement faced a potential crisis of leadership, and could remain true to its roots only so long as those roots restrained any backsliding by the new rulers. Nkrumah's fall was blamed on his failure to remove 'hesitant, faltering or even treacherous associates'. The key moment, James held in retrospect, was Nkrumah's decision to remove his chief justice: 'By this single act, Nkrumah prepared the population of Ghana for the morals of the Mafia. Those learned societies which passed resolutions disapproving of his act

---

* James' name for Kwame Nkrumah.

should have known that Nkrumah could have said the most admirable things about the rule of law. It wasn't that he didn't know. What was important was that he knew all the arguments against such a step and its inevitable consequences.'[215] The alternative had been a very different programme – Lenin's programme from 1921: break up the old state, educate the peasantry, more democracy.

James tended to explain the apostasy of his former allies in terms of their inability to hold fast to a strategy of popular involvement in the struggle. It was ultimately a question of political will. The future of Africa would be determined as if by a political tug of war. At one end were the powers, who wanted to recreate the social relationships of the old colonial regimes. At the other end, were the black masses who resisted them daily. Caught in between were the black leaders. Their failure was a failure to hold their nerve, to restore and deepen the struggle even once independence had been achieved. How then could the leaders secure their ascendancy over the colonial powers? James explanation was social-psychological. The failure of the Caribbean Revolution was a result of the timidity of the island's middle classes: 'I do not know any social class, which lives so completely without ideas of any kind. They live entirely on the material plane ... They aim at nothing. Government jobs and the opportunities which association with the government gives allow them the possibility of accumulating material goods. That is all.'[216]

If it was as simple as to say that the middle-class champions of independence had no commitment to social liberation, then why had James worked so closely with several of the same leaders? What was it about the Caribbean or the African middle classes that exposed them to corruption? In different epochs, the middle classes had led revolutions, 1649 in Britain, 1776 in America, 1789 in France. What then had changed?

Another possible approach to the problem posed by James could be to say that politics in Europe and Africa were not quite as different as they seemed. In both continents, the propertied classes in the cities had long been hostile to working-class demands. In Europe this process can be dated back to 1917, or possibly even to 1848 (Marx's turning-point:

the support of the French middle-class for the violent suppression of a movement to guarantee the unemployed work). In Africa, the transition occurred later but was alike irreversible. James would accept that analysis of Europe. His dissent was to portray developments in other countries as working to a different logic. But why should the propertied in former colonial societies be different from their European counterparts? If the real social question was always class, then surely James' alliance with Nkrumah was misconceived. Would he not have done better to start building the independent movements of workers and peasants not after liberation but long before it?

In the 1950s and 1960s, James shied away from developing a full analysis of the post-colonial societies. In early periods he had shown no such reticence. He had already developed such a critical theory in response to the rise of Stalinism. It is also true that in his early book *The Black Jacobins*, James had shown a greater interest in class relationships outside Europe. James by no means worshiped Toussaint L'Ouverture, nor did he present him without criticism, but presented his grandeur alongside his vacillations and mistakes. 'Toussaint,' James writes, was 'self-contained, impenetrable and stern, with the habits and manners of the born aristocrat. His major error was the neglect of his own people. They did not understand what he was doing or where he was going. It was dangerous to explain, but still more dangerous not to explain.'[217] This last sentence pre-empts the criticisms C L R James would levy at Kwame Nkrumah, and others of his generation, some 30 years later.

One answer could be to revisit Trotsky's argument, as developed by James in the 1930s. For Trotsky claimed, as we have seen, that any Russian revolution would inevitably fail unless it spread to the richer countries of Western Europe. Trotsky and Lenin's worst fear was of a military defeat, that British, French, German or American tanks would be sent in to crush the revolution. But revolutions could also be defeated from within, and decisively. The Russian Revolution did not turn out like the Paris Commune; it was destroyed rather by the rise of Stalin, one of the revolt's minor protagonists. That indeed was the sharp point of James' theory of state capitalism; to argue that even an internal defeat might be fatal to a revolutionary struggle. Could a similar process occur in a post-colonial society; or to reformulate the same question, was it realistic to hope for socialism in Trinidad or Ghana without an equal revolution in the West?

By the early 1960s, James had withdrawn from the positions that he and Trotsky had developed 25 years previously. New activists developed similar ideas, in isolation from the older tradition, but reaching the same conclusions. Frantz Fanon, for example, from the experience of the Algerian revolution, could write: 'The overwhelming majority of nationalist parties show a deep distrust toward the people of the rural areas ... The country people are suspicious of the townsman ... Inside the nationalist parties, the will to break colonialism is linked with another quite different will: that of coming to a friendly agreement with it.' Fanon's solution was a second struggle, a class war rather than a national war: 'Without that struggle, without that knowledge of the practice of action, there's nothing but a fancy dress parade and the blare of the trumpets. There's nothing save a minimum of readaptation, a few reforms at the top, a flag waving: and down there at the bottom an undivided mass, still living in the middle ages, endlessly marking time.'[218]

In Britain and America, lazy thinkers tended to assume that James was simply the elder representative of the new generation of African radicals, variously associated with the labels 'Black Power' or 'Black Consciousness'. Given the opportunity to speak for himself, James did not hesitate to mark the differences between himself and many members of the young generation. James did not see the black population of Britain and America as inherently united, but as divided by class. He did not see black British people as united by a common experience of exile, going back to slavery, and before that to a common origin in Africa, and he did not hold that white people were inevitably hostile to black liberation. In his memoir, *Street Fighting Years*, Tariq Ali describes the 1967 Dialectics of Liberation conference in London, at which James was a mere presence, while the dominant figure was Stokeley Carmichael, the

American advocate of Black Consciousness. 'James hardly raised his voice that day, but he was heard in silence by an audience which had enthusiastically cheered Carmichael. An epitome of classical scholarship, he proceeded without much effort to demolish the black nationalist case, while defending their cause. He did so elegantly, but without mercy. Sitting there listening to this black man with white hair I found myself agreeing entirely with his approach to the question. There could not have been a better antidote to Carmichael, and when James sat down to modest applause, he had after all, been swimming against the tide that day, I applauded loud and long in order to express my gratitude.'[219] A similar distinction between Nkrumah's cause and that of his people eluded James, before it was too late.

Through the 1970s and 1980s, C L R James regularly addressed audiences of radicals in Britain, Europe and right across the world. In the 1970s, his ideas were discussed in Italian magazines including *Quaderni Rossi*. He also taught at Washington DC's Federal City College. Again, however, we can note a certain dissonance between James and the coming generation. Invited to teach in Washington's department of Black Studies, C L R James expressed his pleasure that such a faculty existed. Yet he went on to explain that the invitation had caused him some difficulty. 'I do not know, as a Marxist, Black Studies as such. I only know the struggle of people against tyranny and oppression in a certain social and political setting, and particularly during the last two hundred years. It is impossible for me to separate Black Studies from white studies in any theoretical point of view.'[220]

James' name was made among younger activists, who adopted cultures and politics different from his own. In the same way that black consciousness was alien to him, so too were the cultural references of many young Caribbeans. America was an increasing influence for them, marked by the rise of baseball on the islands at the expense of cricket. For black Americans, in turn, Africa had long been a touchstone, since the days of Garvey and before. Where America went, the Caribbean was sure to follow. James' Trinidadian consciousness, however, saw Africa as no root. 'I pay a lot of respect to Africa', James told one interviewer, 'I have been there many times. I have spoken to many Africans. I have read their literature. But we of the Caribbean have not got an African past. We are black in skin, but the African Civilisation is not ours.'[221]

While often expressing doubts in strategies adopted by others on the left, James refused to be cowed by the defeats around him. He remained a Marxist, insisting that 'the idea that the emancipation of the workers will be the work of the workers themselves is the literal and total truth'.[222] The two most important forces that James identified as capable of bringing direct democracy into life were the workers of Europe and America, and the oppressed black masses of the Caribbean, Africa and North America. Here is James speaking to a British audience, on the occasion of his 80th birthday; 'The socialist basis of society ... is right here in England ... The [workers] are disciplined, united, organised by the very mechanism of the process of capitalist production itself. That is socialism. There is the development of the mechanical means of production. We have them all around us. And at the same time, we have a working class growing in numbers and disciplined, united, organised by the very mechanism of the process of the capitalist production. That Marx says cannot continue. There comes a stage when that conflict explodes.'[223]

To the same audience, James identified the Polish Solidarity movement as an expression of the socialism in which he believed. Solidarity was a movement with no leaders, 'the mobilisation of the great mass of the population'.[224] It was a continuation of the Paris Commune, an expression of the continuing demand for freedom. As with the Hungarian uprising, so with Solidarity: both demonstrated the possibility of spontaneous movements overthrowing even the most brutal dictators (Solidarity's subsequent demise, and the part played by leaders such as Lech Walesa, suggests an over-optimism on James' part).

James was often seen as one of the world's leading exponent of a 'black Marxism', but in many places, he held back from assuming this role. At a meeting in Brixton in 1981, members of his audience asked James to reflect on the racism of English workers. James was more upbeat. Towards the end of his last talk, James was asked for the umpteenth time to comment on the hostility of the unions towards black workers. 'We are sitting here to seek a positive way,' he replied: 'You will have problems, I have seen them. I still have problems. But you have to fight against them and you can be certain if you keep on fighting you win people over to you. If you are not getting support something is wrong with you but if you keep on, as I have found, you keep on, and things come to you.'[225] James did not refute the fears that were quoted at him, rather he listened, and in some ways he endorsed them. But to that audience he made clear that his ideal was a world where black and white could ally.

The key, once again, is cricket. An 1975 article in the *Washington Post* declared Willie Mays the baseball star to be above all a 'black athlete', 'he ran black, swung black and caught black'. In London, James disagreed. Gary Sobers, he argued, was not a great black cricketer, but simply a great cricketer. 'Does Sobers bat, bowl and field black? He plays the game of powers emancipating themselves in a field that needs emancipation.' In writing the piece, James was also guided by the recent news of the death of his old friend, Learie Constantine. 'He died when I specially needed to talk to him ... I believe that Constantine would have been an ally against these racial ideas, benign as they may appear.'[226]

That same summer saw cricket's first world cup, won in balmy sunshine by the West Indies at Lord's. Clive Lloyd scored 102, and Australia were bowled out 18 runs short of victory. A young black British crowd (with more than a few willing white allies) stormed the pitch to celebrate. Drums and whistles were everywhere. The analysis of *Beyond a Boundary,* that free cricket, insurgent and multi-racial, could be created from outside the sport's traditional metropolitan centres, seemed to be vindicated, gloriously, in the field.

8

From a Room Carved of Books

(Previous page) A burnt-out car in Railton Road in Brixton following the 1981 riots. James spent the last years of his life in Railton Road.

We can divide C L R James' political work into two parts. In the first period, which lasted from his arrival in London in 1932 to his return from America in 1953, James was engaged in theoretical work of a preparatory nature. During these years, James formulated the ideas with which we best associate him, including his deep trust in the working class and the black liberation movements, as the two forces charged with the task of bringing the new society into being. In the second period, it seemed that James enjoyed opportunities to move from preparation to leadership. A number of his friends took up positions as founders of parties or even of states, including Eric Williams and Kwame Nkrumah. It looked as if the last decades of James' life were to be marked by a new series of advances. Yet reality failed to match up to the possibilities. James' political ideas became less influential, and while his literary reputation grew undiminished, something had been lost.

The campaigns that interested James were the movements of workers' councils, a system of direct democracy with the maximum emphasis on mass participation and popular decision-taking. James insisted on 'the always unsuspected power of the mass movement'.[227] But the generosity in James' thinking was of a dual character. Most often, it helped him to grasp the possibilities waiting in a situation was closed and hopeless to other activists. At other times, though, the same optimism of the intellect left him vulnerable, as when social movements passed their peak. In James' thinking capitalism had a constant tendency to become dictatorial state capitalism. It became consistently better organised, more vicious and harder to resist. Meanwhile the opponents of capitalism were also always prepared and always equally willing to fight. In this context, the words of James' last piece of fiction and first political essay, 'Revolution', seem prescient, 'If they had landed and taken the city and shown they had guns, they would have had a big following at once. All the people would have been with them.' 'All the people are with us': James was in no sense an anarchist,[228] but he shared with the thinkers of classical anarchism a reluctance to consider the factors that might explain why in one moment protest is all-pervasive and in another period it declines.

There were other ways in which James' contributed to his own isolation. The very quality of James' dissidence lay in the grand sweep of
his Marxism. One interviewer, David Widgery, praised the older man
in the following terms: 'He moves from ancient Greece to the Detroit
auto plants, and then to Florence, in as many sentences.'[229] Yet this real
strength was at other times a weakness. Faced with the dilemmas of
real life, James could formulate answers that were surprisingly abstract.
Trotsky himself made a similar point in criticising James' *World Revolution*. He told James that it was a 'very good book', but that he had noticed
the 'lack of dialectical approach, Anglo-Saxon empiricism, and formalism which is only the reverse of empiricism.'[230] The most telling phrase is
'formalism'. Trotsky detected in James a tendency to discuss real people
and changing personal experiences as if they were categories to be fitted
into boxes (philosophy X, error Y), without a need to understand the
historical dynamics at work in people's lives.

The fiercest critics were also full of praise. 'To the best of my ability',
Widgery wrote, 'I have tried not to hero-worship this man, who if
Marxists believed in such things, would be the greatest living Marxist.'
Widgery met C L R James for the first time at the Mayfair Hotel in
central London on the eve of James' 80th birthday.* These were Widgery's reservations, 'He has been insufficiently consistent in applying his
own criteria for socialist self-emancipation to Nkrumah, Castro and
other revolutionary nationalists. His devastating critique of "vanguard"
parties, those toy Bolsheviks who ape and misunderstand Lenin's politics, is in danger of writing off altogether the need for the sinews of
socialist organisation.' Against such criticisms, Widgery also listed the
many grounds for tribute, 'this is very small beer beside one's respect,
admiration and affection for a revolutionary intransigent who inhabits
both classical and Marxist culture like a familiar home.'[231]

---

* A writer, journalist, doctor and activist, David Widgery (1947–92) was an editor
of *Oz* magazine and a prominent member of Rock Against Racism and the Anti-
Nazi League.

Part of James' genius was to attract around him people of talent, who recognised in their friend something they knew and liked in themselves. George Padmore, Kwame Nkrumah and Eric Williams all fit into this category. So too do life-long activists of the stature of Grace Lee, Raya Dunayevskaya and Selma James, as well as his younger allies Darcus Howe and Linton Kwesi Johnson, and others who could be counted among James' friends: V S Naipaul briefly, the writers Richard Wright, Ralph Ellison and Chester Himes and George Lamming, the historian E P Thompson. Among the sportsmen, Learie Constantine and Frank Worrell could hardly be excluded.

Into this group David Widgery fits as one of the leading activists in the late 1970s protest coalition of Rock Against Racism (RAR) and the Anti-Nazi League (ANL), an alliance of socialists and young punks who took on the party which was then the main carrier of organised racism in Britain, the National Front, and contributed to its defeat. 'You don't have to read James to be a Jamesian', writes Max Farrar, a participant in the anti-Nazi movement. which he insists, was James' politics applied: 'RAR's decision to call its all-day events "carnivals" nicely evokes those moments in Caribbean carnivals at which deeply radical lyrics are sung, anti-establishment satires enacted, and even insurrectionary acts may take place, moments which, of course, James had celebrated.'[232]

C L R James spent his final years in Brixton. With his restless intelligence, James began but failed to complete biographies of various artists, of Shakespeare, and of several of his contemporaries. He continued to lecture, and to write on race, class and cricket, especially for the journal *Race Today,* edited by his nephew, the journalist Darcus Howe. Friends suggested that he should write a new memoir, but each draft showed only James' inability to escape from the narrative that he had already constructed in writing *Beyond a Boundary.* What remains are only fragments. This, for example, is James on the failure of his first marriage: 'I could tell [Juanita] nothing because I had only the vaguest idea of what she was speaking about. It seemed that as a husband, living in the same house, I was most unsatisfactory. Not sexually nor in my behaviour. I am a well-behaved person, I don't quarrel or shout at people, far less shout at my wife. We go out periodically when there is something we want to do, we have friends, there has always been enough money to carry on the affairs of the household, though at times things were rather sharp. But it seems that as a husband, my wife in Trinidad had spotted it. And my first wife in Trinidad was quite plain about it. My virtues as a husband were entirely negative.'[233]

While James' experience of 1960s London had been one of isolation, by the early 1980s he was much in demand. He spoke regularly on public platforms, appeared on the BBC and Channel 4, and was even invited to speak on Radio 4's 'Thought for the Day'. In Hackney, a library was named in James' honour. The latter celebration took place in 1985, just as the council was closing many of its other services.

James' last decade saw the West Indies enjoy their greatest period of sporting triumph. In 1984, 1986 and 1988 England teams were defeated in three successive series. Before 1984, and in all Test history, only four full series of five games had been won by any team by a 5-0 margin. In 1984, the West Indies triumphed 5-0 in England, in 1986 they won 5-0 in the West Indies, and in 1988, they won 4-0 in England again, with one drawn test. The team's and the crowd's thrill in outdoing their former masters was evident at every turn. James celebrated the victories, but he asked his readers to recall also the greatness of several of the earlier West Indies' sides. The present should not be allowed to overwhelm the past. As for England, he detected a 'pervading sickness' in the team's cricket and in British society, but declined to make a full diagnosis.[234] The caution of James' analysis has echoes of his previous scepticism in face of Bradman's triumphs. True achievement is a matter of aesthetics not statistics, and of finding a worthy opponent. James believed in contest, so he felt that this West Indies team would establish its lasting greatness not by repeated blackwashes, but in overcoming some equal rival.

In the midst of these defeats, England were able to win back the Ashes from Australia. James' penultimate piece of cricket journalism was published in 1985. Its subject was Botham, and the all-rounder's part in England's victory. 'Botham's hitting is regulated according to custom and in the tradition of the great orthodox batsmen. He is not exact orthodox. A great batsman never is. The infallible sign of greatness is that somewhere in his method he is breaking the rules, or if not rules, the practices of his distinguished equals. Where Botham is different is that he does not want the real half volley ... I suspect that he prefers the ball a little shorter than the half volley because Botham is hitting sixes and consciously lifting the ball to do so.' The piece ended prematurely. 'Let no one think that an article of a few hundred words can deal with Botham. There will be plenty more later.'[235] One last article appeared: a comparison of Botham and Gower.[236]

Had he been willing to conclude a revised *Beyond a Boundary* with one final chapter, then perhaps C L R James might have ended the book with Viv Richards' team, taking pleasure in their exuberance with the bat, the ball and in the field, and commenting on the relationship between Richards and his audience. The end of direct colonial rule was still within the memory of the older members of the side. Richards had encountered racism for himself as a player in England.[237] History, politics and sport were combined in the West Indies' victory. James, the artist, had all his favourite material at hand. It is a small tribute, though, to James' generosity of spirit, that his last pieces of cricket writing were dedicated not to the West Indies in their pomp but to the star player in the rival team.

Among James' books were studies of Michelangelo, Leonardo, Rapahel, Cezanne, Monet, Picasso and Jackson Pollock. 'Although he often complained that he had to sleep in the same room as his books', Jim Murray recalls, 'I knew each morning when I picked my way over the scattered volumes of Shakespeare, Thackeray or Arnold Bennett which lay around his bed, that they had been his companions during the long hours of darkness.' Another anecdote sets James at home in April 1983, 'I was watching the news with James in his room in Brixton, London. A mass meeting of five thousand British Leyland workers in the north of England voted to continue their walkout over management's abolition of the three minute wash-up time between shifts. The wash-up time was a forty-year tradition at the plant, but it had never been mentioned in a contract. During the report, James pointed to the telly, "Look! Look! Look at that!" I looked, there were the workers massed in the courtyard of the plant; there was the female reporter in the foreground, explaining the vote. I thought, Ah ah! A perfect Jamesian story, industrial workers self-organizing, the issue being not money but quality of life, the story coming to us live from a different part of the country, ordinary people taking everyday history into their own hands. But James continued, "Jim, look! Look at that!" He impatiently leaned forward, touched the upper left corner of the screen. "Look, the steeple, the hills in the distance, the sky." He was referring to the depth of the camera's view, the undivided totality of the picture coming to us on such a small box. He said nothing about the story.'[238]

In his final year, writes Anna Grimshaw, the artist Margaret Glover drew James' portrait, and the image became the focus of James' continued reflections on the sources of his own creativity, 'During the last few months, C. L. R., an insomniac for most of his life, began to sleep. His books lay unopened as he slept deeply, sometimes throughout the day, in his armchair. I slept too. On many afternoons I crept across the room to nap on his bed, feeling the slow fading of his life almost as a sapping of my own strength. But there were moments of happiness, such as a whole day devoted to Beethoven or to a Mozart opera. The room filled with music, the scores laid out across his lap and those bright eyes, alert and curious, as C L R found a companion for his journey into the world of the creative imagination. On the day he died, C L R got up for an hour and sat in his armchair. Although he was slipping in and out of sleep, I watched his eye, through force of habit, drifting back to the portrait, "Why me?" He had often said, seeking rhetorically the answer to life's unique course.'[239]

9

In Retrospect

(Previous page) Cyril Lionel Robert James (1901–89).

As time goes on, C L R James' life and views become ever more relevant. The advocate of colonial revolt has been honoured by the placing of a blue English Heritage plaque near his old home on Railton Road in Brixton. The catalogue of the British Library in London, by no means a complete source, gives us some sight of the growing demand. The first biography of James, it records, was published in 1976, when James was already well into his seventies. Two further biographies followed in the 1980s. In the ten years following James' death, another ten critical studies appeared. Another ten books were published in just five years from 2000, and the rate of production has increased since then. More and more is being written about James. So which face of James should be seen?

According to one early biographer, Paul Buhle, C L R James 'has been an important West Indian novelist, a keen sports critic, Pan-Africanist theorist and spokesman of great pioneer importance, and a philosopher of universal scope'. For Aldon Lynn Nielsen, 'Cricket and books were the parameters' of James' 'lifelong pattern'. The description is incomplete. Better is a line from Scott McLemee, 'To read James is an exercise in rediscovering the world, and an invitation not just to interpret it, but also to change it.' Better still is Jim Higgins' memory of his friend. James' 'best writing was clear, simple and persuasive, and no Marxist in this century wrote better. As a speaker, he was in the highest class ... He was also a good man.'[240] Kent Worcester suggests that James should be remembered as 'an unorthodox left-wing thinker and writer who responded to changing political and social conditions with creativity and verve'. Paul le Blanc describes James 'as one of the most original Marxist thinkers'. Asked to assess his own career, James emphasised its political heart: 'My contributions have been, number one, to clarify and extend the heritage of Marx and Lenin. And number two, to explain and expand the idea of what constitutes the new society.'[241]

C L R James' life spans almost the entire 20th century. When they look back at those hundred years, future generations will surely judge that this period marked a turning point in human history. Any man or woman born in 1500 or 1800 would surely have been forced to accept (if perhaps reluctantly) the truth of Christ's bleak aphorism that the poor will always be with us. By 2000, however, it was no longer clear that the majority of people had any need to live in fear of early death through hunger or disease. Conditions of living that were previously open only to the richest, were now within the reach of many. So while in earlier times, the story of human existence was a question of how science, medicine, and industry could shape a future where plenty was available; the question at the century's end was rather how differently we could order society to answer problems of human affluence, to stop a world set on heating, poisoning, and burning itself to an end? The immediate task was the one James saw, to establish thorough-going democracy. Within months of James' death, the Berlin Wall fell. Popular uprisings like those of 1989, however, can vanquish any dictator, but what to do when the rule is one of abstractions rather than people? How can you vote against speed-up at work worsened by self-exploitation, downsizing, relocation, unemployment and environmental degradation?

The longer answer, James would have argued, could be found in politics and also in cricket. The pleasure of *Beyond a Boundary* lies in the force of this argument, which at first discovery is genuinely surprising; just like the realisation that someone else shares your guilty secret (the discovery proves that there was no need for guilt after all). Most times cricket *is* pastoral, it is indeed backward-looking. Most often it does serve to conceal conflict between people. As practiced at Queen's, the game was seen a hymn to empire. In the classic novel of the 19th century public school, *Tom Brown's Schooldays*, cricket is defined as 'the birthright of British boys, old and young, as *habeas corpus* and trial by jury are to British men'.[242] More than a century later only a few English courts still practice trial by jury,* while habeas corpus is subject to so

---

* In Britain in 2005, less than 2 per cent of all criminal cases were dealt with by juries, *Judicial statistics (revised) England and Wales for the year 2005* (Department of Constitutional Affairs, London: 2006) p 136.

many exceptions that where it is most needed it barely exists at all. But James lived before in an age before the War on Terror, at a hinge in time between the Rugby of Thomas Arnold and our own day.

For James, cricket had a message of potential militancy. The events of his own life seem to prove him right; from Larwood's rejection of bodyline to the emergence of the West Indies team under Clive Lloyd and Viv Richards. Perhaps the best example of cricket working in this fashion comes from apartheid South Africa, where there were absolute distinctions between white and black teams, and this rule was but a part of a wider, legal structure in which different races were forbidden by law from eating, drinking, playing or sleeping together. South Africa's white international team was subject to increasing protests. 'No normal cricket', the placards read, 'in an abnormal society'. In the townships, activists in the South African Council on Sports organised networks of non-racial teams, and the mere existence of mixed sides such as Maritzburg's Aurora was a potent challenge to the government policy of complete segregation.[243] And if resistance can be found in such a concealed location as two batsmen dressed in whites, then truly, joyfully, it must be everywhere.

C L R James' death came on 31 May 1989, following a brief chest infection. Darcus Howe took his body back to Trinidad and he was buried at Tunapuna Cemetery, close to where he had been born. James had insisted that there should be no religious ceremony. The Oilfield Workers Trade Union organised the final rites. Tributes were read. A steel band played Stravinsky's *Rite of Spring* and the *Internationale*. James' monument is a four-pointed gravestone in the shape of an open book. One of its pages displays a single passage from *Beyond a Boundary*: 'Time would pass. Old empires would fall and new ones take their place, the relations of countries and the relations of classes had to change, before I discovered that it is not quality of goods and utility which matter, but movement; not where you are or what you have, but where you have come from, where you are going, and the rate at which you are getting there.'

Notes

Thanks to Anne Alexander, Ian Birchall, Keith Flett, Christian Hogsbjerg, Dave Pinnock and Leo Zeilig for reading the manuscript and suggesting valuable lines of further research. All errors are my own.

1. As Edward Thompson writes, 'the clue to everything lies in his proper appreciation of the game of cricket'. E P Thompson, 'C L R James at 80', in P Buhle (ed.), *C L R James and His Work* (Alison and Busby, London: 1986) p 249; C L R James, *Beyond a Boundary* (Serpent's Tail, London: 1994 edn).
2. F Dhondy, *C L R James* (Pantheon Books, New York: 2001) p 60.
3. 'Introduction', in S R Cudjoe and W E Cain, *C L R James: His Intellectual Legacies* (University of Massachusetts Press, Amherst: 1995) pp 1–22, 1.
4. M Marquese, *Anyone but England: Cricket, Race and Class* (Two Heads Publishing, London: 1998) pp 50–9.
5. S Moss (ed.), *Wisden Anthology 1978-2006: Cricket's Age of Revolution* (Wisden, London: 2006) pp 1202–3.
6. F Dhondy, *C L R James,* p 1.
7. J Murray, 'The Boy at the Window', in G Farred (ed.), *Rethinking C L R James* (Blackwell Publishers, Oxford: 1996) pp 205–18; A Grimshaw, *The C L R James Archive: A Reader's Guide* (C L R James Institute, New York: 1991) p 48.
8. C L R James to Constance Webb, July 1944, quoted in P Henry and P Buhle (eds), *C L R James's Caribbean* (Duke University Press, Durham, NC: 1992) p 21
9. James, *Beyond a Boundary*, pp 7, 9–10; R Ramdin, *From Chattel slave to wage earner* (Martin Brian and O'Keefe, London: 1982) p 11.
10. K Worcester, *C L R James: a political biography* (State University of New York, Albany: 1996) p 5.

11. A Grimshaw, 'Remembering C.L.R. James', talk given to C L R James Society's April 2000 conference on James at Brown University, Rhode Island.

12. James, *Beyond a Boundary*, pp 3, 7.

13. C L R James to V S Naipaul, September 1963, in C L R James, *Cricket* (Alison and Busby, London: 1989) pp 130–3.

14. James, *Beyond a Boundary*, pp 25–6.

15. James, *Beyond a Boundary*, p 16.

16. James, *Beyond a Boundary*, p 47.

17. Grimshaw, *The C L R James Archive*, p 48.

18. Dhondy, *C L R James*, p 5.

19. Dhondy, *C L R James*, p x.

20. James, *Beyond a Boundary*, p 4.

21. A E Horner, *From the islands of the sea: Glimpses of a West Indian Battalion in France* (Nassau: Guardian Office, 1919).

22. James, *Beyond a Boundary*, pp 41–2.

23. James, *Cricket*, p 121.

24. Dhondy, *C L R James*, p 9.

25. S McLemee, 'C L R James: A Biographical Introduction', *American Visions* (April–May 1996).

26. Dhondy, *C L R James*, p 9.

27. James, *Beyond a Boundary*, pp 29, 42.

28. James, *Beyond a Boundary*, p 27.

29. James, *Beyond a Boundary*, pp 27–8; Worcester, *James*, p 8.

30. Williams was also the author of an important Marxist history of slavery, which was influenced by James' study of the Black Jacobins. E Williams, *Capitalism and Slavery* (André Deutsch, London: 1964).

31. James, *Beyond a Boundary*, p 34.

32. James, *Beyond a Boundary*, p 53.

33. H Pine-Timothy, 'Identity, Society and Meaning: A Study of the Early Stories of C. L. R James', in Cudjoe and Cain, *C L R James*, pp 51–60, 55.

34. P Buhle, *The Artist as Revolutionary* (Verso, London: 1988) p 29.

35. J D Young, *Socialism since 1889: a biographical history* (Pinter Publishers, London: 1988) p 184; Dhondy, *C L R James*, p 32.

36. James, *Cricket*, p 158. The French translates as 'without fear and without reproach'.
37. C Webb, *Not without love* (Lebanon, New Hampshire: University Press of New England, 2003) p 202.
38. K Worcester, 'A Victorian with the rebel seed: C L R James and the politics of intellectual engagement', in A Hennessy (ed.), *Intellectuals in the Twentieth-century Caribbean* (Macmillan, Basingstoke: 1992), pp 115–31, 118.
39. C Robinson, *Black Marxism* (University of North Carolina Press, Chapel Hill: 2000) p 255; Grimshaw, *The C L R James Archive*, p 50.
40. 'C L R James, West Indies cricket', *The Cricketer* (6 May–24 June 1933).
41. R A Hill, 'In England 1932-1938', in Buhle (ed.), *C L R James and His Work*, pp 61–81, 64; S Hall, 'A Conversation with C L R James', in Farred, *Rethinking*, pp 15–44, 17.
42. C L R James, *The Life of Captain Cipriani: An Account of British Government in the West Indies* (Colton, Nelson, Lancashire: 1932).
43. James, *Beyond a Boundary*, p 116.
44. Figures from cricinfo.com, correct as of 1 January 2006.
45. Dhondy, *C L R James*, p 33; A Grimshaw (ed.), *Special Delivery: the letters of C L R James to Constance Webb* (Blackwell, Oxford: 1996) p 35; James, *Beyond a Boundary*, pp 114–5.
46. A Grimshaw, *The C L R James Reader* (Blackwell, Oxford: 1992) pp 43–8.
47. *Nelson Leader*, 10 June 1932. I am grateful to Christian Hogsbjerg for this reference.
48. *Nelson Leader*, 8 July 1932.
49. James, *Cricket*, p 241; the story is also told in L Constantine, *Cricket in the Sun* (Stanley Paul, London: 1946) pp 118–9.
50. G Howat, *Learie Constantine* (Allen and Unwin, London: 1975) p 79.
51. R McKibbin, *Classes and Cultures: England 1918-1951* (OUP, Oxford: 1998) p 332.
52. Thanks to Ian Birchall for the story.
53. H Larwood, *The Larwood Story* (London: W. H. Allen, 1965) p 122.
54. D Mayall, 'Rescued from the Shadows of Exile: Nellie Driver, Autobiography and the British Union of Fascists', in T Kushner and

K Lunn (eds), *The Politics of Marginality* (Frank Cass, London: 1990) pp 19–39.

55. C L R James, 'The Nucleus of a Great Civilisation', *Port of Spain Gazette*, 28 August 1932.

56. Nor in P Sagar, *Chronicles of the Pendle Picture Palaces* (Mercia Cinema Society, Wakefield: 2000).

57. The details of the strike I have taken from Bessie Dickinson's unpublished biography of James Rushton. There is a copy in the special collection at Nelson library.

58. A Richardson (et al), *C L R James and British Trotskyism* (Socialist Platform, London: 1987) p 2; James, *Beyond a Boundary*, p 122.

59. Young, *Socialism since 1889*, p 184; Dhondy, *C L R James*, p 32.

60. C L R James, *The Life of Captain Cipriani*; Grisham (ed.), *James Reader*, p 61; C L R James, *The Case for West Indian Self Government* (London: Leonard and Virginia Woolf, 1933).

61. L Constantine, *Cricket and I* (Philip Allan, London: 1933) pp 136–9.

62. Young, *Socialism since 1889*, p 186.

63. O Spengler, *The Decline of the West* (Oxford University Press, Oxford, 1932 edn.) p 396.

64. A Bogus, *Caliban's Freedom: The Early Political Thought of C L R James* (Pluto, London: 1997) pp 28–9. James's influences are also discussed in B Schwarz and S Hall, 'Breaking Bread with History: C L R James and the Black Jacobins', *History Workshop Journal* 46 (1998) pp 17–32.

65. L Trotsky, *The History of the Russian Revolution* (Pluto, London: 1985 edn.).

66. Young, *Socialism since 1889*, p 190.

67. Karl Marx's complex attitude towards colonialism is sympathetically discussed in D Renton, *Marx on Globalisation* (Lawrence and Wishart, London: 2001) pp 81–104. There is a more hostile analysis of Marx's writings in E W Said, *Orientals* (Routledge and Keegan Paul, London and Henley: 1978) pp 153–6; D Geary, *Karl Kautsky* (Manchester University Press, Manchester: 1987) pp 46–59; E Bernstein, *Evolutionary Socialism* (Independent Labour Party, London: 1909) p 196.

68. Some of the tensions of this process are described in G Perrault, *A Man Apart: the Life of Henri Curial* (Zed, London: 1987).

69. 'French Intellectuals and Democrats in the Algerian Revolution', in F Fanon, *Toward the African Revolution* (Penguin, London: 1970) pp 86–101.

70. 'C L R James', in D Widgery, *Preserving Disorder* (Pluto, London: 1989) pp 122–7, 123.

71. The most important source for James' views on cricket is *Beyond a Boundary*. Meanwhile, James' *Guardian* articles can be found in James' collection, *Cricket*. For the *Guardian* in this period, G Fadden (ed.), *The Guardian Century* (Guardian, London: 1999); C L R James, 'The Greatest of all Bowlers: an impressionist sketch of S. F. Barnes', *Manchester Guardian*, 1 September 1932.

72. C L R James, 'Bradman's Remarkable Century at Scarborough', *Manchester Guardian*, 10 September 1934.

73. C L R James, 'Chances of West Indies in the First Test', *Port of Spain Gazette*, 15 June 1933.

74. H Mad. Buckles, *The Development of West Indies Cricket* (Pluto, London: 1998) p 53.

75. James, *Beyond a Boundary*, p 188.

76. James, 'Chances of West Indies in the First Test'.

77. L Constantine, *Cricket in the Sun* (Stanley Paul, London: 1946) pp 56–8.

78. Cited in Buckles, *The Development of West Indies Cricket*, p 71.

79. James, 'Chances of West Indies in the First Test'.

80. Richardson, *C L R James and British Trotskyism*, p 4.

81. Worcester, *James*, p 48.

82. E Manning, *Comrade O Comrade, Or Low Down on the Left* (Jerrold's, London: 1947) p 134.

83. Richardson, *C L R James and British Trotskyism*, p 5.

84. C L R James, 'Is this worth a war? The League's scheme to rob Abyssinia of its Independence', *New Leader*, 4 October 1935.

85. Richardson, *C L R James and British Trotskyism*, p 3.

86. P Dorn, 'A Controversial Caribbean: C L R James', lecture delivered in spring 1995 at the San Francisco Art Institute.

87. P Robeson Jnr, *The Undiscovered Paul Robeson* (Wiley, London: 2001). A version of the text of James' play is given in Grimshaw, *James Reader*, pp 67–111.

88. R A Hill, 'In England 1932-1938', in Buhle (ed.), *C L R James and His Work*, pp 73–4.

89. C Hogsbjerg, 'C L R James and Italy's Conquest of Abyssinia', *Socialist History* 28 (2006) pp 17–37, 30.

90. C L R James, *Monty Alley* (Secker and Warburg, London: 1936).

91. A Richardson, 'Introduction', in C L R James, *World Revolution 1917-1936* (Humanities Press, London: 1993 edn).

92. C L R James, 'Lancashire Collapse at Aigburth', *Manchester Guardian*, 20 June 1935.

93. McLemee, 'C L R James: A Biographical Introduction'.

94. L Cripps, *C L R James, Memories and Commentaries* (Cornwall, London: 1997) pp 30, 32–3,

95. Cripps, *C L R James*, pp 48, 65, 80.

96. James, *Cricket*, pp 53–5.

97. C L R James, *The Black Jacobins: Toussaint L'Ouverture and the San Domingo Revolution* (Secker and Warburg, London: 1938) pp 3–4.

98. James, *The Black Jacobins*, p 108.

99. James, *The Black Jacobins*, p 147

100. James, *The Black Jacobins*, p 279.

101. *Morning Post*, 3 February 1803; James, *Beyond a Boundary*, p 119.

102. There is a very effective alternative history of Wilberforce's politics in R Blackburn, *The Making of New World Slavery: from the Baroque to the Modern 1492-1800* (Verso, London: 1999).

103. James, *The Black Jacobins*, p 67.

104. McLemee, 'C L R James: A Biographical Introduction'.

105. G Farred, *What's my name? Black vernacular intellectuals* (University of Minneapolis Press, Minneapolis: 2003); A Dupuy, 'Toussaint-Louverture and the Haitian Revolution: A Reassessment of C L R James' interpretation', in Cudjoe and Cain, *C L R James*, pp 106–17.

106. B Souvarine, *Stalin* (Secker and Warburg, London: 1939 edn); C L R James, *A History of Negro Revolt* (Independent Labour Party, London: 1938).

107. McLemee, 'C L R James'.

108. Dhondy, *C L R James*, p 72.

109. C L R James letter to Constance Webb, 1945, cited in R D G Kelley, *Freedom Dreams: the Black Radical Imagination* (Beacon Press, Boston: 2002) p 49.

110. A Shawki, 'Black Liberation and Socialism in the US', *International Socialism* 47 (1990) pp 3–112, 61.

111. G Breitman (ed.), *Leon Trotsky on Black Nationalism and Self-Determination* (Pathfinder Press, New York; 1967) pp 40–8.

112. D Widgery, *Preserving Disorder* (Pluto, London: 1989) p 124.

113. Young, *Socialism since 1889*, p 185.

114. C L R James, 'Cricket is losing a supreme artist', *Glasgow Herald*, 17 August 1938.

115. James, *Beyond a Boundary*, p 191.

116. Richardson, *C L R James and British Trotskyism*, p 14.

117. G L Boggs, 'C L R James: Organising in the United States 1938-1953', in Cudjoe and Cain, *C L R James*, pp 163–72, 165.

118. C Webb, 'The Speaker and his Charisma', in Buhle, *C L R James and His Work*, pp 168–77, 169.

119. Webb, *Not without love*, p 74.

120. Grimshaw (ed.), *Special Delivery: the letters of C L R James to Constance Webb*, p 51.

121. Webb, *Not without love*, p 81; A Grimshaw, 'Special Delivery: The Letters of C L R James to Constance Webb, 1939-1948', in Farred, *Rethinking*, pp 45–74, 56.

122. Grimshaw, *The C L R James Archive*, p 55.

123. Webb, *Not without love*, pp 85–6.

124. Young, *Socialism since 1889*, p 200.

125. Webb, *Not without love*, p 132.

126. Webb, *Not without love*, pp 123–4

127. Webb, *Not without love*, p 132.

128. C L R James et al., *The Invading Soviet Society* (Johnson-Forest Tendency, New York: 1947).

129. L Trotsky, *The Revolution Betrayed: What is the Soviet Union and where is it going?* (Pathfinder, New York: 1972 edn) p 249.

130. Resolution submitted by C L R James (writing as 'J. R. Johnson') to the 1941 convention of the Workers Party of the United States.

131. 'In other senses' should arguably read 'in other hands'. Another writer influenced by James was the Palestinian Trotskyist Tony Cliff, living in Britain after 1946. Cliff would develop his own theory of state capitalism, one grounded in economic as well as political analysis. Yet the debt to James is evident, not least in Cliff's references to 'the invading Soviet society': T Cliff, *Stalinist Russia: A Marxist Analysis* (Mike Kidron, London: 1955) p 222 and elsewhere.

132. C L R James, *Notes on Dialectics* (Alison and Busby, London: 1980 edn); J Rees, *The Algebra of Revolution* (Routledge, London: 1999) passim.

133. James, *Notes on Dialectics*, p 85.

134. James, *Notes on Dialectics*, p 36.

135. D Renton, *Classical Marxism* (New Clarion, Cheltenham: 2002) p 140.

136. Bogues, *Caliban's Freedom*, p 26.

137. James, *Notes on Dialectics*, pp 212–13.

138. Webb, *Not without love*, p 134.

139. Webb, *Not without love*, p 162

140. Webb, *Not without love*, pp 176, 202, 207, 253.

141. P Le Blanc, 'C L R James and Revolutionary Marxism', in S McLemee and P Le Blanc, *C L R James and Revolutionary Marxism* (New Jersey: Humanities Press International, 1994) p 16.

142. C L R James, *Every Cook Can Govern: A Study of Democracy in Ancient Greece* (Correspondence, Detroit: 1956) p 2.

143. James, *Every Cook Can Govern*, p 3.

144. D Renton, *Dissident Marxism* (Zed, London: 2003); Bogues, *Caliban's freedom*; 'Do I contradict myself? / Very well then I contradict myself, / (I am large, I contain multitudes)', W Whitman, *Song of Myself* (Penguin Books, London: 1999) section II, lines 1314–1316.

145. For more on the planned biography of Shakespeare, see Grimshaw, *The C L R James Archive*, pp 15–18.

146. James, *Beyond a Boundary*, pp 19, 44.

147. C L R James, *American Civilisation* (Blackwell, Oxford: 1993) pp 29, 31, 106.

148. James, *American Civilisation*, pp 205, 260.

149. C L R James, *Mariners, Renegades and Castaways: The Story of Herman Melville and the World we Live in* (Bewick, Detroit: 1978 edn) p 36.

150. C L R James to Saul Blackman, 15 June 1952, quoted in Grimshaw, *The C L R James Archive*, p 86.

151. Worcester, *James*, p 118; G Lamming, *Natives of My Person* (Longman, London: 1972)

152. V S Naipaul, *A way in the world* (Vintage, London: 2001) p 130. Also Worcester, *James*, p 174. James' 1980 verdict on Naipaul is revealing: 'I have long suspected that the worship they (English and American intellectuals give to him is something that corresponds to a deep inner corruption in them.' Grimshaw, *C L R James Archive*, p 13.

153. C L R James to Grace Lee and Selma Weinstein, 14 December 1953, quoted in Grimshaw, *The C L R James Archive*, p 89.

154. Richardson, *C L R James and British Trotskyism*, p 17.

155. C L R James, *The Nobbie stories for children and adults* (University of Nebraska Press, Lincoln: 2006). Worcester, *James*, p 121.

156. Dhondy, *C L R James*, p vii.

157. James, *Cricket*, pp 71–3.

158. D Scott, 'The Sovereignty of the Imagination: An interview with George Lamming', *Small Axe* 6/2 (2002).

159. P Fryer, 'Hungary in Retrospect', *New Reasoner* 1 (1957) pp 71–7; J D Young, *The World of C L R James: the Unfragmented Vision* (Clydeside Press, Glasgow: 1999) p 2.

160. R Dunayevskaya and G Lee, *State Capitalism and World Revolution* (Charles H. Kerr Publishing Company, Chicago: 1986 edn).

161. Grimshaw, *James Reader*, p 263; Worcester, *James*, p 139.

162. M Haynes, '1956 Hungary's revolution: the rebirth of socialism from below', *International Socialism Journal* 112 (2006) pp 81–107, 88.

163. C L R James, *Facing Reality* (Facing Reality, Detroit: 1967) pp 106–7.

164. C Hogsbjerg, 'Beyond the Boundary of Leninism? C.L.R. James and 1956', paper given to conference on 1956, London, Institute of Historical Research, February 1956; C L R James, *Nkrumah and the Ghana Revolution* (Allison and Busby, London: 1977) p 70.

165. James D Young suggests that there were various knots of followers of James in the Socialist Review Group and in its successor, the

International Socialists, the first groups of James-ians emerging in the mid-1960s and the second leaving in 1969. Young, *The World*, pp 11, 259–60.

166. Ramdin, *From Chattel slave to wage earner*, pp 135–8.

167. E Williams, *Capitalism and Slavery* (Andre Deutsch, London: 1964); Hogsbjerg, 'Beyond the Boundary of Leninism?'; S R Cudjoe, *Eric E. Williams speaks* (University of Massachusetts Press, Wellesley, Massachusetts: 1993) p 72.

168. Grimshaw, *The C L R James Archive*, p 59.

169. M Ordaz, *Home coming of a famous exile: C L R James in Trinidad and Tobago* (M Ordaz, Trinidad: 2003) p 5.

170. B Wilson, 'The Caribbean Revolution', in Buhle (ed.), *C. L. R. James and His Work*, p 122.

171. James to ANR Robinson, PNM Representative on the Board of Directors, 7 March 1960, Institute of Commonwealth Studies (ICS) James paper KS 40.

172. *The Nation*, 4 March 1960; J Anderson, 'Cricket and Beyond: the Career of C L R James', *The American Scholar* (Summer 1985) pp 345-62, 359.

173. H Beckles, *The Development of West Indies Cricket. Vol 1, The Age of Nationalism* (Pluto, London: 1998) p 78.

174. James to Michael Manley, 21 August 1959, ICS, James papers, J1.

175. B Ragoonath, 'On West Indian Politics', in B Ragoonath (ed.), *Tribute to a Scholar: Appreciating C L R James* (University of the West Indies, Kingston: 1990) pp 92–112, 101.

176. Memorandum, 29 March 1960, ICS, James papers, F. 1.1.1.

177. 'A Convention Appraisal', in Cudhjoe, *Eric E. Williams Speaks*, pp 327–52.

178. C L R James to Eric Williams, 14 July 1960, quoted in Grimshaw, *The C L R James Archive*, p 93; I Oxaal, *Black Intellectuals and the Dilemmas of Race and Class in Trinidad* (Schenkman Publishing, Cambridge, Mass.: 1982) p 135.

179. C L R James to Mrs. Marguerite Wyke, Secretary, Tribunal of the Disciplinary Committee, 23 March 1961, ICS, James papers, F. 1.1.9.

180. C L R James to 'Arthur', 28 March 1961, quoted in Grimshaw, *The C L R James Archive*, p 94.

181. C L R James, *Modern Politics* (PNM Publishing, Port of Spain: 1960) pp 154–5.

182. Grimshaw, *The C L R James Archive*, pp 24–5; P Buhle, 'Political styles of C L R James: An Introduction' in Buhle (ed.), *C. L. R. James and His Work*, pp 22–9, 25.

183. James, *Beyond a Boundary*, p 18.

184. James, *Beyond a Boundary*, p 7.

185. James, *Beyond a Boundary*, pp 24–5.

186. James, *Beyond a Boundary*, pp 39–40.

187. James, *Beyond a Boundary*, p 122.

188. James, *Beyond a Boundary*, p 153.

189. James, *Beyond a Boundary*, pp 72–3, 196–7.

190. James, *Beyond a Boundary*, p 173.

191. James, *Beyond a Boundary*, pp 175–9, 186–7.

192. James, *Beyond a Boundary*, pp 184, 186–94, 212–22.

193. Marquese, *Anyone but England*, p 8.

194. James, *Beyond a Boundary*, p 105.

195. James, *Beyond a Boundary*, p 126.

196. L Constantine, *Colour Bar* (Stanley Paul, London: 1954) p 26.

197. M Dresser, *Black and White on the Buses: The 1963 Colour Bar Dispute in Bristol* (Broadsides Co-op, Bristol: 1986) p 57.

198. A D Needham, *Using the Master's Tools: Resistance and the Literature of the African and South-Asian Diasporas* (Macmillan, Basingstoke: 2000) p 31.

199. D Walcott, *What the Twilight says* (Faber, London: 1998) p 118.

200. James, *Beyond a Boundary*, p 257; Beckles, *The Development of West Indies Cricket Vol 1*, p 179.

201. P Foot, *Words as Weapons* (Verso, London: 1990) p 224.

202. James, *Beyond a Boundary*, pp 257–61.

203. Young, *The World*, p 259.

204. T Topham (ed.), *Report of the fifth national conference on workers' control* (Institute of Workers' Control, Hull: 1967) p 55.

205. Young, *Socialism since 1889*, p 204.

206. Grimshaw, *The C L R James Archive*, p 41.

207. C L R James, *A History of Pan-African Revolt* (Drum and Spear, Washington, D.C.: 1969) p 117.

208. For more on Rodney's relationship to James, see W Rodney, 'The African revolution', in Buhle (ed.), *C. L. R. James and His Work*, pp 30–48; also Renton, *Dissident Marxism*, pp 139–61.

209. Dhondy, *C L R James*, p 179.

210. James, *Nkrumah*, p 9.

211. M Marable, 'The Fall of Kwame Nkrumah', in Buhle (ed.), *C. L. R. James and His Work*, pp 105–20; James, *Nkrumah*, p 12.

212. P Sedgwick, 'Ghana – another saviour thrown on the scrapheap', *Labour Worker*, 14 March 1966.

213. James, *Nkrumah*, pp 181–8.

214. James, *Nkrumah*, pp 103, 157, 169, 177.

215. James, *Nkrumah*, p 13.

216. B Wilson, 'The Caribbean Revolution', in Buhle (ed.), *C. L. R. James and his Work*, pp 121–30, 124.

217. James, *The Black Jacobins*, pp 147, 240.

218. F Fanon, *The Wretched of the Earth* (Grove Press, New York: 1968) pp 124, 147.

219. Young, *The World*, p 264.

220. Buhle, 'Political styles of C L R James: An Introduction' in Buhle (ed.), *C. L. R. James and His Work*, p 26; Young, *The World*, p 288.

221. James interviewed by Angus Calder, 28 February 1984, Grimshaw, *The C L R James Archive*, p 84.

222. C L R James, *At the Rendezvous of Victory* (Allison and Busby, London: 1984) p 242.

223. C L R James, *80th Birthday Lectures* (Race Today, London: 1981) p 15.

224. James, *80th Birthday Lectures*, p 16.

225. James, *80th Birthday Lectures*, p 71.

226. James, *Cricket*, p 279.

227. 'Letters', in Buhle (ed.), *C. L. R. James and His Work*, pp 153–63, 156

228. Some of James' previous co-thinkers have evolved in that direction, A Harewood and T Keefer, '"Revolution as New Beginning"; an interview with Grace Lee Boggs', *Upping the Anti*, Spring 2005.

229. Widgery, *Preserving Disorder*, p 123.

230. Shawki, 'Black Liberation and Socialism in the US', p 65.

231. Widgery, *Preserving Disorder*, p 123.

232. M Farrar, 'Preliminary notes on the relationship between the work of C L R James and some of the radical black, anti-racist and left movements in the UK, 1970s to 1990s', conference paper, September 2001; also D Renton, *When we touched the sky: the Anti-Nazi League 1977-1982* (New Clarion Press, Cheltenham: 2006).

233. S R Cudjoe, '"As Ever Darling, All My Love, Nello": the love letters of C L R James', in Cudjoe and Cain, *C L R James*, pp 215–43, 216.

234. C L R James, 'The Decline of English Cricket', *Race Today*, January 1985.

235. 'Botham Hitting Sixes', *Race Today*, August-September 1985; for a similar statement of praise, Foot, *Words as Weapons*, pp 223–8.

236. C L R James, 'Botham and Gower', *Race Today*, July 1986.

237. Foot, *Words as Weapons*, p 228.

238. Murray, 'The Boy at the Window', pp 205–18; Grimshaw, *The C L R James Archive*, p 14.

239. A Grimshaw, 'C L R James: A Personal Memoir', in Cudjoe and Cain, *C L R James*, pp 23–33, 31.

240. Buhle, *The Artist*, p 1; A L Nielsen, *C L R James* (University Press of Mississippi, Jackson: 1997) p 171; McLemee, 'C L R James'; J Higgins, *Speak one more time: selected writings* (Socialist Platform, London: 2004) p 137.

241. K Worcester, 'The real C L R James', *Workers' Liberty* 68 (2001); Le Blanc, 'Challenges of a Black Revolutionary'; Shawki, 'Black Liberation and Socialism in the US', p 58.

242. T Hughes, *Tom Brown's Schooldays* (Puffin, London: 1994 edn).

243. A Desai, V Padayachee, K Reddy and G Vahed, *Blacks in Whites: A Century of Cricket Struggles in Kwa Zulu Natal* (University of Natal Press, Pietermaritzburg: 2002).

Bibliography

Primary works in alphabetical order (selection)

A History of Negro Revolt (Independent Labour Party, London: 1938).

American Civilisation (Blackwell, Oxford: 1993).

At the Rendezvous of Victory (Allison and Busby, London: 1984).

Beyond a Boundary (Hutchinson, London: 1963).

The Black Jacobins: Toussaint L'Ouverture and the San Domingo Revolution (Secker and Warburg, London: 1938).

The Case for West Indian Self Government (Leonard and Virginia Woolf, London: 1933).

C L R James and Revolutionary Marxism; selected writings of C L R James 1939–1949 (Humanities Press, Atlantic Highlands: 1994).

The C L R James Archive: A Reader's Guide (C L R James Institute, New York: 1991).

C L R James on the "Negro Question" (University Press of Mississippi, Jackson: 1996).

The C L R James Reader (Blackwell, Oxford: 1992).

Cricket (Alison and Busby, London: 1989).

Essays and Lectures by C L R James: A tribute (University of the West Indies, Mona: 1989).

Facing Reality (Facing Reality, Detroit: 1967).

(with G Breitman and others) *Fighting Racism in World War II* (Pathfinder, New York: 1980).

The Future in the Present: selected writings of C L R James: volume 1 (Allison and Busby, London: 1977).

History of Negro Revolt (Fact, London: 1938).

History of the Pan-African Revolt (Drum and Spear Press, Detroit: 1969).

The Invading Soviet Society (Johnson-Forest Tendency, New York: 1947).

The Life of Captain Cipriani: An Account of British Government in the West Indies (Coulton, Nelson, Lancashire: 1932).

Mariners, Renegades and Castaways: The Story of Herman Melville and the World we Live in (C L R James, New York: 1953).

(with Tony Bogues) *Marxism and Black Liberation: Three Essays* (Hera Press, Cleveland: 1980).

Marxism for our times (Mississippi University Press, Jackson: 1991).

Minty Alley (Secker and Warburg, London: 1936).

Modern Politics (PNM Publishing, Port of Spain: 1960).

Nkrumah and the Ghana Revolution (Allison and Busby, London: 1977).

The Nobbie stories for children and adults (University of Nebraska Press, Lincoln: 2006).

Notes on Dialectics (written 1948, published Allison and Busby, London: 1980).

Party Politics in the West Indies: Formerly PNM, Go Forward (Vedic Enterprises, San Juan: 1962).

Special Delivery: the letters of C L R James to Constance Webb (Blackwell, Oxford: 1996).

Spheres of Existence: selected writings of C L R James: volume 2 (Allison and Busby, London: 1980).

(with R Dunayevskaya and G Lee), *State Capitalism and World Revolution* (Johnson-Forest Tendency, Detroit: 1950).

World Revolution 1917-1936: The Rise and Fall of the Communist International (Secker and Warburg, London: 1937).

The Marxist Internet Archive also has a wide collection of James' articles: http://www.marxists.org/archive/james-clr/index.htm.

Secondary works (selection)

Beckles, H M D, and B Stoddart (eds), *Liberation Cricket: West Indies Cricket Culture* (Manchester University Press, Manchester: 1995).

Bogues, A, *Caliban's Freedom: The Early Political Thought of C L R James* (Pluto, London: 1997).

Breitman, G (ed.), *Leon Trotsky on Black Nationalism and Self-Determination* (Pathfinder Press, New York: 1967).

Buhle, P (ed.), *C L R James: His Life and Work* (Alison and Busby, London: 1986).

——, *The Artist as Revolutionary* (London: Verso, 1988).

Cliff, T, *Stalinist Russia: A Marxist Analysis* (Mike Kidron, London: 1955).

Constantine, L, *Colour Bar* (Stanley Paul, London: 1954).

——, *Cricket and I* (Philip Allan, London: 1933).

——, *Cricket in the Sun* (Stanley Paul, London: 1946).

——, *Cricketer's Carnival* (Stanley Paul, London: 1948).

Cripps, L, *C L R James, Memories and Commentaries* (Cornwall, London: 1997).

Cudjoe, S R, and W E Cain, *C L R James: His Intellectual Legacies* (University of Massachusetts Press, Amherst: 1995).

Dhondy, F, *C L R James* (Weidenfeld and Nicolson, London: 2001).

Fanon, F, *Toward the African Revolution* (Penguin, London: 1970).

Farred, G (ed.), *Rethinking C L R James* (Blackwell, Oxford: 1996).

——, *What's my name? Black vernacular intellectuals* (University of Minneapolis Press, Minneapolis: 2003).

Grimshaw, A, *C L R James; A Revolutionary Vision for the Twentieth Century* (C L R James Institute, New York: 1991).

——, *Popular Democracy and the Creative Imagination: the Writings of C L R James* (C L R James Institute, New York: 1991).

Foot, P, *Words as Weapons* (Verso, London: 1990).

Hennessy, A (ed.), *Intellectuals in the Twentieth-century Caribbean* (Macmillan, Basingstoke: 1992).

Henry, P, and P Buhle, *C L R James' Caribbean* (Duke University Press, Durham, North Carolina: 1992).

King, N, *C L R James and Creolisation: Circles of Influence* (University Press of Missouri, Jackson: 1991).

Mannin, E, *Comrade O Comrade, Or Low Down on the Left* (Jarrolds, London: 1947).

Marquese, M, *Anyone but England: Cricket, Race and Class* (Two Heads Publishing, London: 1998).

McLemee, S, and P Le Blanc, *C L R James and Revolutionary Marxism* (Humanities Press International, New Jersey: 1994).

McClendon, J H III, *C L R James' Notes on Dialectics: Left Hegelianism or Marxism-Leninism?* (Lexington, Boulder: 2005).

Nielsen, A L, *C L R James* (University Press of Mississippi, Jackson: 1997).

Nordquist, J, *C L R James: a bibliography* (Research and Services, Santa Cruz, California: 2001).

Ordaz, M, *Home coming of a famous exile: C L R James in Trinidad and Tobago* (M. Ordaz, Trinidad: 2003).

Ragoonath, B (ed.), *Tribute to a Scholar: Appreciating C L R James* (University of the West Indies, Kingston: 1990).

Renton, D, *Classical Marxism* (New Clarion, Cheltenham: 2002).

——, *Dissident Marxism* (Zed, London: 2003).

——, *When we touched the sky: the Anti-Nazi League 1977-1982* (New Clarion Press, Cheltenham: 2006).

Richardson, A (et al), *C L R James and British Trotskyism* (Socialist Platform, London: 1987).

Robeson, P Jnr., *The Undiscovered Paul Robeson* (Wiley, London: 2001).

Robinson, C, *Black Marxism* (University of North Carolina Press, Chapel Hill: 2000).

Samoiloff, L C, *C L R James: memories and commentaries* (Cornwall Books, New York: 1997).

Sanchi, T A, *C L R James: The man and his work* (T A Sancho, Guyana: 1976).

Schwartz, B, *West Indian Intellectuals in Britain* (Manchester University Press, Manchester: 2003).

Trotsky, L, *The History of the Russian Revolution* (Pluto, London: 1985).

Walcott, D, *What the Twilight says* (Faber, London: 1998).

Webb, C, *Not without love* (University Press of New England, Lebanon, New Hampshire: 2003).

Widgery, D, *Preserving Disorder* (Pluto, London: 1989).

Williams, E, *Capitalism and Slavery* (André Deutsch, London: 1964).

Worcester, K, *C L R James: A Political Biography* (State University of New York Press, Albany, New York: 1996).

Young, J D, *The World of C L R James: the Unfragmented Vision* (Clydeside Press, Glasgow: 1999).

Picture Sources

The author and publishers wish to express their thanks to the following sources of illustrative material and/or permission to reproduce it. They will make proper acknowledgments in future editions in the event that any omissions have occurred.

akg-Images: pp. 92–3; Getty Images: p. 175; Topham Picturepoint: pp. 3, 13, 37, 52–3, 72–3, 118–19, 146–7, 162–3.

Index